WALKING IN
THE FOREST OF BOWLAND

Grizedale Reservoir, Walk 3.5 Photo: R Lowe

WALKING IN
THE FOREST OF BOWLAND

by

GLADYS SELLERS

CICERONE PRESS
MILNTHORPE, CUMBRIA

© Gladys Sellers 1994
ISBN 1 85284 154 0

A catalogue record for this book is available from the British Library.

ACKNOWLEDGEMENTS

I should like to thank my several friends, Mr & Mrs R.B.Evans, Miss A.H.Pilkington, and Mr Walt Unsworth for the loan of various books that have helped my search for information about the historical aspects of the Forest of Bowland. I should also like to thank Miss Pilkington for check walking a large number of these routes for me. In addition I must thank Mr J.Shaw of the County Surveyor's Department for his prompt help in resolving certain right of way path problems.

The maps in this book are drawn by
Martin Collins.

Other Cicerone guidebooks by the author:
Walks on the West Pennine Moors
The Yorkshire Dales
The South Pennines
The Douglas Valley Way
The Ribble Way

Front cover: Dunsop Bridge to Middle Knott with High Laithe
Farm. Photo: Richard Lowe

CONTENTS

The Forest of Bowland, an Area of Outstanding
Natural Beauty 7

The Historic Forest of Bolland 12

A Basic Geology of the Bowlands 17

The Walks 21

            Equipment 21

            Using this Book 22

            Concerning the Walker 22

Chapter 1:   Walks around Chipping and Bleasdale 25

            Beacon Fell Country Park 57

Chapter 2:   Walks around Slaidburn, Dunsop Bridge
            and Whitewell 61

Chapter 3:   Walks around Wyresdale and its Fells 105

Chapter 4:   Walks around the Northern Fringe 125

Chapter 5:   Walks around the Southern Fringe..............144

            Sources 160

Advice to Readers

Readers are advised that whilst every effort is taken by the author to ensure the accuracy of this guidebook, changes can occur which may affect the contents. It is advisable to check locally on transport, accommodation, shops etc but even rights of way can be altered and, more especially overseas, paths can be eradicated by landslip, forest fires or changes of ownership.

The publisher would welcome notes of any such changes.

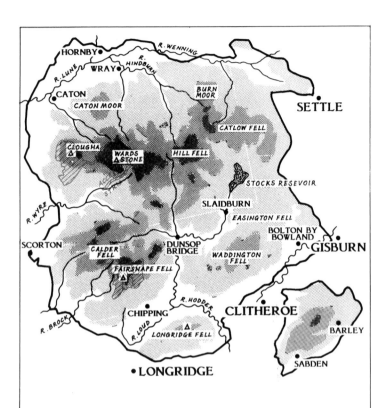

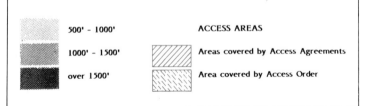

THE FOREST OF BOWLAND AREA OF OUTSTANDING NATURAL BEAUTY

	500' – 1000'	ACCESS AREAS
	1000' – 1500'	Areas covered by Access Agreements
	over 1500'	Area covered by Access Order

The Forest of Bowland

AN AREA OF OUTSTANDING NATURAL BEAUTY

The Forest of Bowland and Pendle Hill were jointly designated as an Area of Outstanding Natural Beauty in 1964. The Pendle Hill part is separated from the main mass of the Bowlands by the Ribble valley, and as it is fully covered in the author's *Walking in the South Pennines*, published by Cicerone Press, no further mention of it is made in this guidebook. The area covered by the modern Forest of Bowland is much larger than that of the historic forest of Bowland, or Bolland to use the old spelling, and includes the former Forests of Wyresdale, Roeburndale and Bleasdale. Where the Area of Outstanding Natural beauty is implied in this book, the spelling "Bowland" is used, or as the area is commonly referred to, the Bowlands. Where the ancient forest is implied, "Bolland" is used.

It is not easy to get a picture of the area covered by the Bowlands. Four sheets, Nos. 97, 98, 102 and 103 of the 1:50,000 Landranger Series are needed, but the old 1924 1" to the mile edition of Ribblesdale does the job almost perfectly, omitting only a trifling fringe in the west. A much more readily available alternative is Bartholomew's ¹/₂" to the mile North Lancashire sheet 31, though obviously it lacks some of the detail of the 1" maps.

None of these maps show the boundary of the Area of Outstanding Natural Beauty. Starting in the north-east, its boundary coincides with that of the Yorkshire Dales National Park from Clapham to Settle, from where it swings westwards to omit the flatlands of the Ribble valley and a chunk of the less interesting landscapes to the west of it, then snakes away south-east through Tosside to the outskirts of Gisburn. Then it follows the line of the A59 towards Sawley and diverts from it to include that village together with the villages of Grindleton, West Bradford and Waddington. Some little distance west of Waddington it turns south in order to encompass Hurst Green and Longridge Fell, but turns north-west before it reaches Longridge, cutting over the end of Longridge Fell, and continues in that direction almost to the M6.

The boundary then wriggles northwards between the fells and the M6 until it crosses the Lancaster-Kirkby Lonsdale road where it swings north-east to include a small area north of the Lune valley. Finally it turns due east to Clapham passing close to Hornby and Wennington, but omitting Low and High Bentham. Most roads carry a sign, "Forest of Bowland" when they enter the Area. This Area of Outstanding Natural Beauty is 803 square km or 312 square miles in extent, by far the greater part of which is the area known to walkers as "The Bowlands".

The Forest of Bowland AONB, comprises several quite different and contrasting types of landscape. The main mass of gritstone capped fells with their large expanses of peat moorland is one of the last remaining wilderness areas of England. Here are grandeur and remoteness, the hand of Man barely visible, whilst in the Pennines it is scarcely possible to escape the world of cars and mill chimneys. The lower valleys of the Rivers Hindburn and Roeburn are well wooded, whilst the valleys of the Rivers Loud and Hodder are more open. This is where a large part of the rather sparse population is found - only around 13,000 people in 1981. The upper part of the Hodder valley beyond Slaidburn is, however, quite different, being heavily forested. The Gisburn Forest is no successor to the mediaeval deer forest as it consists mainly of conifers planted on the water catchment area of Stocks Reservoir. Only ornithologists have a good word to say for conifer plantations these days, and Gisburn Forest is an important habitat for goshawk, sparrowhawk, long-eared, tawny and barn owls, as well as smaller birds such as siskins, goldcrest, pied flycatchers and tits. The island in the adjacent Stocks Reservoir provides a nesting site for waders, wildfowl and gulls, and the remoteness of the moors makes them an important breeding ground for many upland birds besides grouse: ring ouzel, golden plover, curlew and short-eared owl, also some of the rarer falcons.

The moorlands support some characteristic plant communities of mosses and rare flowering plants mainly of interest to the botanist, though for the tourist and walker the heather is one of the glories of the Bowland fells in late summer. Unnoticed by most walkers are the old hay meadows, mostly around Slaidburn, that have never been ploughed and re-seeded. These have a wide range of grass varieties, some of them rare, and they are becoming increasingly rare because of economic pressures resulting in re-seeding. It is worth noting that there are fourteen Sites of Special Scientific Interest in the Bowlands.

Any landscape which is an Area of Outstanding Natural Beauty is a national asset which must be conserved mainly by being left undisturbed. It follows that these areas are managed in a rather different way from the National Parks, one of whose prime requirements is to promote the enjoyment of the countryside for quiet recreation. In an Area of Outstanding Natural Beauty recreation takes second place but is not neglected. Tourism keeps a low profile: there is no single Tourist Information office that serves the entire area, though that in Clitheroe (tel: 01200 25566) covers the Chipping to Slaidburn to Tosside area as it lies within the Ribble Valley. Lancaster's Tourist Office (tel: 01524 841656) covers the Wyresdale area. There is not a lot of choice of accommodation: some farms do bed and breakfast and there are a number of village pubs, but few holiday cottages. There has been a youth hostel at Slaidburn since 1946 to the author's personal knowledge, but it is the only one. Though a simple hostel at today's standards it is very well used.

A recent development of interest to the walker and cyclist is the camping barns. These are a joint venture involving the YHA, the Countryside Commission, the Long Distance Walkers Association, the Ministry of Agriculture and the Rural Development Commission and offer basic accommodation, little more than a stone tent with a water supply and flush toilet, not to be confused with the bunkhouse barns of the Yorkshire Dales. They usually sleep 12 to 15 people in unisex sleeping. In the Forest of Bowland there are camping barns at:

Clarkhouse Farm, Chipping. It is on the road to Parlick Pike, $1/2$ mile from the village.

Greengore Farm, Hurst Green. It is a good mile out of Hurst Green, probably best reached by its access road that leaves the minor road between the Punch Bowl and Hurst Green.

Upper Brow Top Farm, Quernmore near Lancaster. It is on the Trough Road, steeply up the hill for about $3/4$ mile from Quernmore Post Office.

Those at Downham (Clayhouse Farm) and Giggleswick (Grain House) are close enough to be useful to some people. All these

9

can be booked by contacting the Bowland Camping Barns Reservations Office, 1a New Market Street, Clitheroe, BB7 2JW (tel: 01200 28366).

There is a caravan and campsite at Edisford Bridge, Clitheroe and another at West Bradford.

The vast majority of walkers are day visitors needing somewhere to park their cars, for public transport is so limited as to be worth very little to the walker. For the record, Burnley and Pendle bus services run a service from Clitheroe to Settle via Waddington, Whitewell, Slaidburn and Tosside. Ring Clitheroe (01200) 28985 for the times. Scorton has an occasional bus service and Dolphinholme is served from Lancaster. Chipping has a relatively good service from Preston via Longridge. Those walkers who live in Lancashire will find bus timetable leaflets in their local tourist information office whose address is given in the telephone directory.

The Ribble Valley Rail runs from Clitheroe calling at Whalley, Langho, Ramsgreave and Wilpshire, and Blackburn to Manchester Victoria, Piccadilly and Airport. It is an hourly service, but does not run on Sundays. It is hoped eventually to extend the service to Leeds.

A number of car parks have been made so as to discourage roadside parking which cuts up grass verges and causes traffic congestion on the roads in summer: the drive through the Trough must be one of the best known scenic drives in Lancashire and a big tourist attraction. The Lancashire County Council runs a Countryside Ranger Service as does the North West Water Authority in their catchment areas. That said, little attention has been paid to the other amenities the walker in our National Parks has come to expect. Although there is a good network of right of way footpaths on the low ground especially in the Hodder Valley and Bleasdale, the walker will find wobbly stiles aplenty, even collapsed and missing ones here and there, few footpath signposts and a dearth of waymarks in many places. That said, the Bowlands Countryside Service is working with the County Surveyor (who has the statutory duty of ensuring that footpaths are unobstructed) to improve the general situation, and indeed, during the time it has taken to prepare this guidebook, waymarking has greatly improved and a number of stiles have been repaired in the Chipping area.

On the other hand, there are few right of way tracks over the Bowland Fells yet many bulldozed tracks with "Keep Out" notices, more than in any other moorland area of Britain. It is small consolation that there are two access areas which give a most valuable increase in the amount of moorland walking. They are the fruits of sixteen years of frustrating negotiations between the Lancashire County Council and the landowners and occupiers. In them the walker is free to wander as he or she pleases: over close cropped grass or wet black peat hags, to have purple heather brushing his or her feet and to enjoy the rocky bracken covered slopes of Clougha. A superb narrow access strip, a mere 12 metres wide, runs over Grit Fell and Ward's Stone, at 1,836ft (561m) the highest point in the Bowlands, to Tarnbrook, and gives one of the best walks in the Bowlands. The other access area is on the fells above Chipping, some 1,500 acres of it covering Parlick Pike, Fair Snape and Wolf Fell. Would that there were more of them, or that the Ward's Stone access strip could be extended to Wolfhole Crag and the Hornby road!

In return for freedom to wander in these access areas certain byelaws and access restrictions must be observed. These are displayed at all the main access points, a bit late in the day when you are already there. Most importantly, dogs are not allowed except on Wolf Fell where they must be kept under proper control, and fires and stoves are prohibited. In addition the access areas (but not Fair Snape) and the access strip are closed on some days during the grouse shooting season. These days are known well in advance and can be had from the Head Ranger, telephone Forton (01524) 791075. In dry summers the areas may be closed because of the fire risk.

It is unfortunate that neither these access areas nor their car parks are shown on the Ordnance Survey maps. However, a leaflet which shows them may be obtained from the Estates Department, Lancashire County Council, East Cliff County Offices, Preston PR1 3EX or from any of the rangers. In greater detail, with grid references for those who can handle such things, the Clougha Access Area has car parks at Jubilee Tower (on the Trough road from Lancaster) GR 542574; Birk Bank, Quernmore, GR 526604; and Little Cragg, Littledale, GR 546618. There is no car park at Tarnbrook at present. Fair Snape, Wolf and Saddle Fells do not have any car parking areas except at Chipping. Those at Beacon Fell Country Park are rather too distant to be useful for the latter access area.

The Historic Forest of Bolland

There is very little evidence as yet of prehistoric man in the Bowlands. The best known site is the early Bronze Age village sometimes known as a "Woodhenge" in Bleasdale. Fairy Holes, a cave across the Hodder from Whitewell yielded early Bronze Age remains when it was excavated in 1946. No doubt others will come to light, but early men of whatever date were extremely thin on the ground in Bolland.

The Romans seem to have been the first people on the scene in any numbers though they did not colonise the area nor build a fort, but a military road. Its course is clearly shown on the 1:25,000 maps, going right across the fells from their fort at Ribchester to the one at Burrow in Lonsdale, part of the main route from their major fort at Chester to Carlisle. True to type it runs in a straight line over the fells changing direction from time to time to ease the gradient as on Jeffrey Hill, or to locate a river ford or maintain the correct general direction. Its line, usually a vague ridge, can be seen in many places by the observant walker, but in most places it has been incorporated into modern tarmac roads or farm access roads.

Briefly, the road left Ribchester in a north-westerly direction crossing Longridge Fell at Jeffrey Hill, slanting down the hillside to Brookhouse Farm, the first place where its ridge can be clearly seen today. It then crossed the Hodder near Doeford Bridge, changed direction slightly and crossed Browsholme Heights, where it is incorporated in the modern road. Yet again it changed direction slightly, and dropped down towards Croasdale, Slaidburn. The well known Hornby road over the fells from there takes the course of the Roman road over the moor but leaves it at about the high point to drop off to the right into the head of Hindburndale, through Ivah and on to cross the River Wenning between High and Low Bentham where it enters the Lune valley and leaves the Bowlands.

The Anglo-Saxon invaders of the sixth and seventh centuries colonised the limestone areas around Whitewell and Slaidburn which provide better feed for sheep than the grasses that grow on the fells. Place name evidence shows that the Vikings were there too, arriving from their colonies in the Isle of Man and Ireland in the eighth and ninth centuries and colonising the higher ground on the fringe of the Hodder valley for their sheep farms. There are a great many farm names derived from Norse family names in the area. For example, the farm of Beatrix above Dunsop Bridge was once called Batherarges, the same word ending "argh" as appears in Grimsargh and Goosnargh. Inevitably the Norman take over of Anglo-Saxon England was complete in Bowland as elsewhere, and Domesday Book (AD 1086) records that Roger of Poitou held the manor of Grindleton and that it had the following townships: West Bradford, Waddington, Bashall, Mitton, Hammerton, Slaidburn, Battersby (Beatrix today), Newton, Bogeworth, Easington, Radom and Sotleie. Evidently the Hodder and Ribble valleys were well settled by that time.

Nevertheless, the greater part of England was heavily wooded (except the high ground). This woodland was principally oak, ash, alder, holly, and hazel in the north and contained many open glades. Even in Henry VII's time more than half of England was still forest. In Norman times much of England's forested ground was hunting forest or chases, all of them exclusively for the benefit of the nobility, and many reserved for the king. These were known as Royal Forests or Chases. The Area of Outstanding Natural Beauty known as the Forest of Bowland comprises several of these former forests owned by various of the nobility. The Bolland Forest's boundaries, starting at Chipping, went south to the River Loud, then to the Rivers Hodder and Ribble, to Bolton Brook, Threap Green, through the present day Gisburn Forest, north to Austwick common, then west across Bolland Knott to Cross of Greet, curling round the heads of Whitendale and Brennand to the Grey Stone of the Trough, from where it looped round Langden Head and Burnslack to run due south to Chipping.

Abutting on to the north-west boundary of Bolland Forest was the Wyresdale Forest whose boundary swung north from the Grey Stone of the Trough to Wolfhole Crag then along the watershed to Grit Fell and south-west to Dolphinholme where it turned south to reach the boundary of the Bolland Chase on Hayshaw Fell. There were two smaller chases, the Quernmore Forest and the Roeburndale

Forest, which abutted onto the northern boundary of the Wyresdale Forest, and Bleasdale Forest abutted onto the south-western side of Bolland Forest, stretching as far north as Oakenclough.

These forests were all subject to special laws aimed at preserving certain animals for hunting, usually red and fallow deer, wild boar and wild cattle. These formed an important source of food for the upper classes, as well as giving the excitement of the chase. Many restrictions were placed upon the inhabitants of the various settlements along their boundaries. Peasants were not allowed to hunt or take deer by other means such as running them down with dogs. As some safeguard, the peasants' dogs had to be small enough to pass through a dog stirrup, otherwise they had their front paws cut off. A dog stirrup is preserved in Browsholme Hall. The peasants were not allowed to enclose their land in order to protect their crops from the deer, nor could the animals be molested in any way. Peasants were not allowed to take timber from the forests for building, (though they could take firewood,) probably to discourage the clearing of the fringes of the forest round the villages and converting the land into fields. Note that Slaidburn including Hammerton, and Newton were never part of the forest. The Forests had their own special courts held twice yearly to deal with these and other offences such as theft and trespass. Bolland's was held at Whitewell, its administrative centre, and Wyresdale's at Marshaw.

By the middle of the thirteenth century the demand for cattle had increased, and coupled with the nobility's need for a bigger cash income from their land, caused the establishment of a large number of cattle farms or vaccaries in the area. Cattle were used for ploughing because, although slower than horses, they could be worked harder. The horse was the preserve of the nobility for use when hunting or in battle. The great majority of the farms shown on today's maps were originally vaccaries in the bigger clearings in the forest. The cattle were long horned shaggy beasts, hardy enough to withstand most winters. The herds are thought to have contained 70-80 animals, and ranged free in the clearings in the forest or on the high fells, safeguarded by a stockman who lived in a simple wooden hut. Calder Dyke, high on Bleasdale Fell, is thought to be part of the stockade of one of the cattle enclosures.

Inevitably the number of deer decreased and to help in their conservation for hunting, two deer parks were established in the Forest of Bolland, Leagram Park and Radholme Park, the first near Chipping, the second across the River Hodder close to Whitewell and adjoining Browsholme. The parks were made by enclosing several hundred acres of land with a ditch 4ft deep and 8ft wide and using the earth to build a ridge which was topped with oak palings. The deer were not hunted within the parks which were havens of security for them, inhabitants of an early conservation scheme of a different sort, for the deer were turned out into the forest whenever the local lord wanted to hunt. Parks of this type were commonly built during the thirteenth century and were abandoned or disparked in the sixteenth, Leagram in 1556 when it was sold to Richard Shireburne of Stoneyhurst. The vaccary system of farming had ended about a century earlier as the tenant population of the villages increased. The Forest of Bolland remained part of the Crown lands until the Restoration of Charles II who gave it to General Monk and created him Duke of Albermarle.

Although organised hunting of deer ceased with the end of the Royal Forest, deer remained in secluded parts and so to this day, though these are sika deer, not the original red and fallow deer. There are thought to be around 140 of them in the Slaidburn area, shy creatures, frequenting woodland not the open fell. As in many upland areas the lesser nobility and landed gentry established sporting estates during the eighteenth and nineteenth centuries, principally for grouse and pheasant shooting. The preservation of the birds and their shooting rights became important and ordinary men had no access to the land as is shown by this printed announcement, dated 1828, by the Duke of Buccleuch, then at Browsholme: "...all his tenants should assist as far as they are able, the Keeper and Bowbearer of the Forest of Bolland, in preserving GAME; and are hereby requested to warn off and discharge every person that may come onto their separate farms without the written leave of His Grace or the Bowbearer."

Thus were sown the seeds of today's very limited access to the fells in the modern Forest of Bowland, but many other factors have aided this unfortunate fact of life. In rural areas a network of paths grew up taking people from farmstead to farmstead, village to village, often going direct over the moors. There were few farms and even fewer villages in Bolland. The Industrial Revolution, starting as it did in the countryside, caused even more paths to be established by people going to work - but it hardly touched the Bowlands except on the western fringes, though Chipping is probably near enough to Preston and Longridge to have been affected by developing industry there. Early tourism played its part in the development of footpaths in the Yorkshire Dales, aided by the publication of guidebooks after the opening of the Settle and Carlisle Railway in 1876, but the railways gave Bowland a miss. By the late 1920s and early 1930s when the rambling movement really took off, the vested interests of the wealthy landowners, concerned for their grouse and pheasant shooting rights, were immovable. In all fairness it must be stated that shooting makes a considerable contribution to the landscape and economy of the Bowlands today. The glory of the heather covered fells in August is maintained by the springtime rotational burning of old heather, a technique developed to produce new shoots for grouse to feed on, and new heather flowers better than old woody stuff. The moors and fells would loose much of their attractiveness were they not heather clad.

Parlick from Beacon Fell, Walk 1.9

A Basic Geology of the Bowlands

Any observant walker in the Bowlands will have noticed distinctive whitish limestone outcrops by the River Hodder at Slaidburn and that the walls around Whitewell are made of limestone. Assuming he/she has walked in the Bentham area, he/she will be aware that there are no limestone outcrops there and the rocks are the same sort as those of the fells themselves. The curious ones will wonder what happened to cause the Slaidburn-Hodder area to be different.

The immediate answer is that the limestone around Slaidburn and Whitewell is part of the Clitheroe Anticlyne. These rocks are the oldest to be found in the Bowlands and were laid down some 350 million years ago at the bottom of a warm shallow sea. Millions of tiny shell clad organisms lived in them and when they died their shells formed a sediment at the bottom of the sea. From time to time they were mingled or layered with mud and became a number of slightly differing limestones. The oldest and lowest one is the dark Chatburn limestone and above it are the Worston and Bowland Shale Groups, the first very rich in lime. Aeons of time later the climate changed, the tropical seas disappeared and a huge river that drained a large part of the Northern Hemisphere developed in its place, laying down a variety of sandy sediments in its delta. These sediments became the shales, sandstones and gritstones of our northern uplands of which the Bowlands are a part.

This long phase of sediment deposition came to an end as a period of mountain building known as the Armorican orogeny started. It caused a great upheaval in the rock structures of the north of England raising them to form a wide asymmetrical arch known as the Pennine Anticline as well as several subsidiary ones including the Lothersdale and the Clitheroe Anticlines. Some 280 million years later, after all these overlying rocks had been weathered away, the River Ribble flowed along the top of one of these lesser anticlines. In due course Clitheroe was built there and the anticline was given the town's name by geologists. Now anticlines, being gentle curves, have their opposite number, synclines. The Chatburn limestone now starts to dip and forms a syncline deep below

WALKING IN THE FOREST OF BOWLAND

ground under Waddington and Easington Fell's sandstones (and beneath Pendle on the other side of its apex) and reappears at the surface again round Whitewell and Slaidburn as another smaller anticline. The rocks dip again and a still smaller anticline brings the limestone to the surface at Sykes to the east of the Trough road.

Another minor limestone feature in Bowland is the reef knolls, far more prominent around Clitheroe than in Bowland itself. They are of a quite different limestone, very rich in coral fossils, and are thought to have developed only in shallow places in the tropical seas at a time when a large amount of mud was present in the water, for they are always found on top of rocks of the Worston Shale Group. The largest reel knoll, Worsaw Hill near Clitheroe, stands 200 feet above the surrounding countryside. The reef knolls in Bowland are very much smaller and are clustered around Whitewell on both sides of the River Hodder and on the banks of the Hodder below Slaidburn. The whole of this series of anticlines and synclines with their reef knolls is part of the Ribblesdale Fold Belt or Craven Basin which extends roughly to the foot of the fells north-west of Slaidburn.

The fells themselves belong to a structural block known simply as the Bowland Block. Concurrentely with the Amorican Period a series of major faults (and many minor ones) ran across the Pennine Anticline dividing it into a number of major blocks of land. The Askrigg Block that makes a large part of the Yorkshire Dales is one of them. Some of these blocks were raised, others dropped down; all of them were tilted to a greater or lesser extent. The Bowland Block is one of these structural blocks and is tilted northwards against the Askrigg block and separated from it by the South Craven fault. It is composed of the Upper and Lower Bowland Shale Group of rocks which includes some sandstones, and is capped with Millstone Grit. One of them, Pendle Grit, forms the summits of the higher ground - including Longridge Fell and Pendle Hill which lends its name to that particular gritstone. Because the rocks of the Bowland Shales and the Pendle Grit were not folded the fell tops are substantially level resulting in large areas of ill-drained peat bog. Their steep sides are due to the easily eroded nature of the Bowland Shales. Even the modest height of Nicky Nook is of Pendle Grit, for it is the top of a minor anticline uplifted by a minor fault. Faulting in the

Pennines is often associated with mineral veins and the minor faults in Bowland associated with the Ribblesdale Folds are no exception. Lead was mined close to Brennand, at Whitendale and at Sykes in the nineteenth century.

Although geological structure is the foundation of scenery the last Ice Age made some changes to the Bowlands landscape. Ice from the Ribble and Lune Valleys and from the Lake District covered the high ground, but because the rocks are not folded they were not heavily eroded and direct glacial action amounted to a rounding of the edges of the fells, rather than the carving of high corries or deep valleys as it did in the Lake District, where the glacial ice tended to follow the folds of the rocks and to exert its biggest effect there. The Bowlands were affected more by the changes that took place during the melting of the ice than by the ice itself.

At its maximum development the main Ribble glacier breached the Hodder-Ribble watershed west of Rathmell and penetrated into the Hodder valley at Slaidburn. This subsidiary glacier was parallel to the main Ribble glacier and Longridge Fell deflected it westwards through the low col at Chipping. It could not escape onto the Lancashire plain because that was occupied by ice from the Irish Sea and the Lake District, but it diverted the Hodder (which used to flow westwards through the Loud valley to the Wyre) to join the Ribble. This diversion explains why the big wide valley separating Longridge Fell and the Chipping Fells is drained only by the little River Loud. Probably the most noticeable feature of the Bowlands attributable to the last Ice Age is the Trough of Bowland. This deeply cut narrow defile was formed by a melt water stream escaping from a lake dammed up by an ice front at the time the glaciers were retreating. It is thought that the ice front was on the Wyresdale side and caused the water to flow *up* the valley on that side and down the Dunsop Bridge side. The ice front also enlarged the cols at the top of the Hornby Road and at the top of the Slaidburn-High Bentham road. On a smaller scale melt water streams of the Lune Valley glacier carved out the deep valley of Windy Clough on Clougha and other similar deep cut valleys in that area.

Glacial sediments were deposited thickly on the lower hillsides and in the side valleys, but drumlins, such a prominent feature of Upper Ribblesdale, are few and far between in Bowland. As the great thaw progressed landslides were frequent in the sodden ground especially from steep escarpments where the softer Bowland Shales are located. The remains of a large one can be seen in the great hollow below Wolf Fell, and there are many others. The ongoing process of weathering since the last Ice Age has caused many parallel deep cut grooves or gullies, now grass grown, on the steeper slopes of the softer Bowland Shales. They are easily seen in the area around Sykes, on the flanks of Wolf Fell and other places.

It is worth knowing that Clitheroe Castle Museum has a first rate display of the geology of the lower Ribble Valley which includes the south side of the Bowlands. Its diagrams and pictures explain the anticline/syncline structrues better than words and its collection of fossils from the reef knolls is second to none. It is open April to the end of October, afternoons only, with a small entry fee.

The Walks

Right of way or permissive and concessionary paths are used throughout in this book. It is always useful to know in advance a bit about what the walks are like, long or short, hard going or not. They are divided into three categories of similar standard to those used in the author's *The Yorkshire Dales: a Walker's Guide to the National Park*, published by Cicerone Press. The easiest, Category C, are short easy walks with not a lot of uphill, suitable for those with young families. There are very few of these in the Bowlands, but Beacon Fell Country Park and Brock Valley Nature Trail are particularly suitable for young children. Category B, by far the largest number, are half-day or short day walks, many of them with some fairly wet or rough going and route finding problems. Category A are more demanding, spending most of the time on the moors and giving a lot of rough wet going, sometimes with route finding problems which, however, tend to be fewer than in the fields. With a few exceptions, once a walker is a field's length or so from the villages, trodden paths disappear leaving him/her dependent on a guidebook, map or other people's knowledge.

Equipment

Category A: good, reasonably waterproof boots are highly desirable. Wear breeches, long trousers or trackster type trousers unless there is a heat wave. Have a windproof jacket or a breathable waterproof that can be worn continuously without sweating. Take a pullover and waterproof overtrousers to supplement the jacket. Long gaiters are almost essential in all except drought conditions. Have a woolly cap, map and compass (and know how to use them) and some food over and above that required for the day.

Category B: use lightweight boots. Modest inexpensive ones will suffice in summer. Have a windproof jacket or a breathable waterproof that can be worn continuously without sweating. Take a pullover and waterproof overtrousers to supplement the jacket.

Category C: all you need for these are trainers or comfortable shoes, and knowing the vagaries of the weather, a waterproof would be prudent. Otherwise, wear what you would wear for a walk in the park that particular day.

In winter all walks go up a category and add to the category A walks an extra pullover, scarf, windproof gloves, thermos with a hot drink, and a bivvy bag.

Using this Book

In deference to the many objections levelled at my use of time instead of miles to indicate the length of a walk I have added the mileage to the preamble of each walk. Mileage alone, in an area like the Bowlands, is quite an inadequate guide to the length of time a walk will take and that is usually the main criterion. It makes no allowance for the height to be made, nor the rough boggy going on the moorland walks, nor route finding difficulties in untracked fields, nor the dodgy stiles and gates so often found. That said, times given in the preamble to each walk are for the slowish to average walker and do not include rests, time for photography and the like. Some allowance is made for route finding problems but much will depend on the walker's own experience of that type of walking. The sketch maps in this book only indicate the general line of the walk and are not intended to replace the relevant 1:25,000 OS map(s) which are a vital tool for walking on the low ground in the Bowlands. The maps required for each walk are given in the preamble to that walk. However, accurate map reading and interpretation is a refined skill that needs a lot of practice, not helped by the changes that have taken place in the countryside since the last survey was made. It is much easier to follow a guidebook, and this book aims to give detailed directions that will keep the walker on route.

Concerning the Walker

Finally, please remember that although these walks use right of way or permissive paths and the access areas, it behoves us to treat the countryside with respect. Do nothing that will hinder the efforts of people who make a living from the land. Do nothing that will injure your environment - leave nothing but footprints, take nothing but photographs - to quote the guide lines of the Sierra Club of America. To be a bit more specific:

1. Take all your litter including tins and bottles home with you.
2. Note that stoves and fires are not permitted in the access areas.
3. Be careful with matches and cigarettes. Moorland fires are devastating.
4. Enjoy the flowers and trees where they are growing.
5. Take care not to pollute any stream. It may provide some farm's drinking water.
6. Close all gates so that animals cannot stray onto the road.
7. Note that in the access areas dogs are not permitted at any time and in other areas keep your dog on a lead in lambing time. A sheep in lamb chased by a dog, even if not touched by it, is liable to loose that lamb.
8. Take care not to block farm gates and access roads by careless car parking.

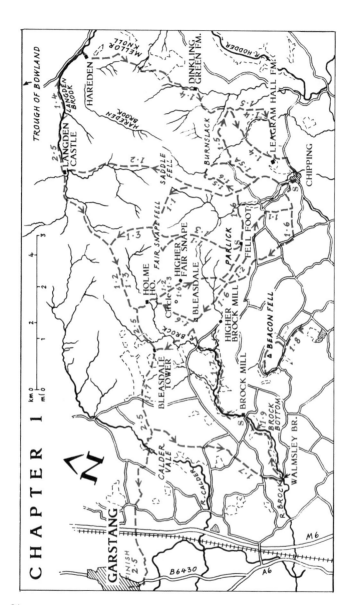

Chapter 1
WALKS AROUND CHIPPING AND BLEASDALE

About Chipping
Walks in the Access Area

1.1	The Access Areas' Skyline,	Category B
1.2	Saddle Fell and Bleadale Water from Chipping,	Category A
1.3	Parlick, Fair Snape Fell, Fiendsdale Head and Bleasdale,	
		Category B+
1.4	The Fair Snape - Langden Castle - Trough of Bowland Circuit,	
		Category A

Other Walks

1.5	Chipping to Burnslack, returning by Lickhurst,	Category B or C
1.6	Along the Foot of the Access Area,	Category B
1.7	The River Brock and Bleasdale,	Category B
1.8	The Brock Valley Nature Trail,	Category C
1.9	Beacon Fell Country Park,	Category C

ABOUT CHIPPING

Chipping has its origin in pre-Domesday book times, for it is mentioned there as Chipenden and belonged to the de Lacy family of Clitheroe. It was not part of the Forest of Bolland but was in Little Bolland, and Leagram Park was a part of the hunting laund in the days of that forest. The village was laid waste in a Scots raid of 1322 and the heart of the village we know today is a result of the development of the woollen cloth trade in the seventeenth century. John Brabin's school in the well named Windy Street is very well known, a fine but modest building in the style of the times, and sets the scene for the heart of the village. John Brabin was first and foremost a Quaker, a wealthy dyer and cloth merchant who never married and made provision in his will for the school which was built in 1684. His will also provided enough money for the uniforms of sixteen pupils and the cost of apprenticing three boys to a trade every year. If that was not enough, he built alms houses for the local poor next door to the school. It is not surprising that his house in Talbot Street (next door to the post office) has an inscription over the door that reads: "Let him that loveth God love his brother also".

St Bartholomew's church stands in a dominant position and although there was a church in Chipping before 1230, most of the present building is nineteenth-century work as it was heavily restored in 1874, when Chipping had developed an industrial base. The church is generally locked, but has a double brass plaque to two wives, who died in 1611 and 1623 respectively, of Robert Parkinson of Fair Snape. The Parkinson family were wealthy landowners in the area at that time and for a couple of centuries afterwards. There is a sundial with the date 1708 set upon stone steps in the churchyard. It is of some interest that John Wesley visited Chipping in 1752 but was given a hostile reception by the population who evidently did not share the independent outlook of the folk of the South Pennines.

Chipping stands on Chipping brook, a vigorous, fast flowing stream of the type so often used for sites of early mills. The 1:25,000 Clitheroe and Chipping map shows three tiny mill ponds, two of them now filled in and used for modern housing sites. The topmost site was almost certainly Chipping's corn mill in medieval times and was still a corn mill in the middle of the nineteenth century. Then one corn mill does not seem to have been sufficient for its needs and there was another in the village itself, which is now a restaurant and has restored the water-wheel. A John Berry, who was the publican of the Sun Inn, established a chair factory by the stream in the 1840s which is still going strong today. Upstream of it there was another factory in the mid nineteenth century, Saunder Rake, now being developed as a housing site. There was a spindle factory at Startifants and further along that road a nail making factory. Nail making was still done by hand and in a community where wood was an important raw material, an important commodity. Chipping must have been a busy industrialised community by the middle of the nineteenth century. It even had a workhouse for its poor and unemployed, a concept abolished by the development of adequate social services. A military camp was built in 1892 somewhere between Chipping and the fells, thought to be somewhere between Parlick and Saddle End Fells, and a firing range was established there. Today Chipping has a free car park, two pubs, post office, and village shop which sells the local Chipping cheese, a cafe and restaurant.

WALKS IN THE ACCESS AREA

Before considering one of these walks you should remember that DOGS ARE NOT ALLOWED in the Access Areas nor may fires be lit or stoves used. The areas may be closed on some days between August 12th and December 31st for shooting or in times of severe drought.

All the walks may be termed variations on a theme, having certain stretches in common, in particular Walks 1.1 and 1.2 use the same starts and finishes at Chipping. Walk 1.3 starts and finishes at Fell Foot, though it could use the same start and finish as walks 1.1 and 1.2 should parking be impossible at Fell Foot. Walk 1.4 reverses the route to Fell Foot from Chipping and has a totally different finish.

THE ACCESS AREAS' SKYLINE   Walk 1.1

This walk is the easiest one of the four that use the access areas of Saddle, Wolf, and Fair Snape Fell as there is less peat bog to deal with, indeed, the walking over both Wolf and Saddle Fells is on a green cart track that gives excellent going. It has some very rewarding views, particularly over Morecambe Bay.

Category: B
Time: 3¹/₂ hours
Distance: 5¹/₂ miles
Maps: Pathfinder Series No.668 Garstang and No.669
             Chipping and Clitheroe (SD44/45 and SD64/74)
Start at: the car park, Chipping. It is well signed and has toilets.

Chipping to Saddle End

Face the church and leave the car park on the left walking up the lane. Take the right fork and continue past the chair works, Chipping's traditional industry. At the bridge you will see the huge beech logs stacked for slitting: on a weekday you may see the job being done and get a whiff of the solvents used in the lacquering process. Continue alongside the mill pond, a relic of the days when the mill took its power from a water-wheel. About half-way along on the right is the start of a drive to a house. The path to Burnslack starts a yard or two along it. It is signed but not too easy to spot. Go steeply up the field then follow the fence to find a decrepit stile. Continue along the line of electricity poles keeping above the hollow track where it drops into the clough, for the stile is not obvious and is well above the stream. From it a clear path leads through the wood to the footbridge.

Given a good day the views of the fells as you walk this length are superb. Parlick is well to the left, then comes the skyline that you are going to walk from right to left, namely Saddle, Wolf and Fair Snape Fells.

Then make up towards the farm and bear left to reach their access road. Follow this to the tarmac road below Saddle End.

Saddle End to Fair Snape Fell

Go straight across and follow the access road past Saddle End Farm and its buildings onto the cart-track up Saddle Fell. After a little while you will come to a gate with the Access Area notice board. Where the track starts to rise again a little way after that gate, it divides and re-joins in a complex fashion. It doesn't matter which part you take so long as you keep away from the right-hand edge: all roads lead to Rome, in this case the stile over the fence ahead. From it a good green cart track climbs gently almost to the top of Fair Snape (1,707ft, 520m), the highest point of the access area, stopping about 200 yards short. The heap of stones marking the summit is well to the right and across a set of peat hags. Pay your respects to it, and if visibility is good, locate Ingleborough to the north-east by its characteristic profile. To its left comes Whernside and further left again Great Coum, and yet again, just the top sliver of the Howgills. To its right is Pen-y-ghent, then Fountains Fell and finally, the indefinite flat top of Embsay Moor.

Now follow the fence in a westerly direction over rather boggy ground to a wooden step stile, then continue to the western top, Fair Snape Fell, marked by a large cairn and trig point. It is a fine view point for the Lancashire coast.

Parlick , Photo: R Lowe

To the north-west Morecambe Bay sits silver-blue at your feet backed by the dark mass of Black Combe whilst other Lake District hills can be made out to the right until they are cut off by the nearer Bowland Fells. Letting your eye move south the River Estuary divides the Fylde from the main Lancashire plain beyond which you may see the Welsh Hills, slate blue and distant.

From it a little path drops gently away and will lead you back to the boundary fence of the Access Area. Simply follow this down all the way to Parlick (1,416ft, 432m), then bear left to follow the steep track down to Fell Foot.

Fell Foot to Chipping

Continue down the lane to the road and straight ahead you will find the stile on the left in about 50 yards. Keep straight across the field to find the next stile and from it bear right a little to find a gate from where you bear left then follow the hollow of the streamlet right down the field to find the stile by the gate onto the road. Turn left and as soon as you have passed the road junction turn right through the farmyard at Fish House Farm and continue along the cart-track into the field. Then keep straight down it aiming just to the right of the barn, cross the little stream and the stile ahead then make straight up the field to a stone slit stile onto a farm road. Straight opposite is another stile. Now head diagonally right across the field to find the next one and then go straight ahead to the centre of the field. Now turn left and keep straight on to enter the farm yard. Turn right on the road to reach Chipping in 5 minutes.

SADDLE FELL AND BLEADALE WATER FROM CHIPPING
Walk 1.2

This varied and demanding walk uses the same start as Walk 1.1 to Saddle End, then crosses Saddle Fell into Bleadale, a wild and little visited valley, and descends to Langden Castle. From there it returns to the western side of the fells by the right of way path over Fiendsdale Head and to Chipping by field paths.

It is arguably the most demanding shortish walk in this book having two major ascents - by Bowland's standards - three river crossings and a long stretch of trackless rough heather moorland to cross as well as a bit of compass work and careful map reading thrown in. For these reasons it is graded A and is not recommended on a bad day because of problems at the river crossings. N.B. The path down Bleadale is *not* a right of way path but is shown on OS map No.669. A.A.Lord claims that there is no objection to walkers using it.

Category:	A
Time:	about 6 hours
Distance:	10 miles
Maps:	Pathfinder Series No.669 Clitheroe and Chipping, No.668 Garstang and No.660 Slaidburn and Forest of Bowland (SD64/74, SD44/54 and SD65/75) The last of these locates Langden Castle but only covers about ¾ mile of the route and is hardly necessary.
Start at:	the car park, Chipping.

Chipping to Saddle End

Face the church and leave the car park on the left walking up the lane. Take the right fork and continue past the chair works, Chipping's traditional industry. At the bridge you will see the huge beech logs stacked for slitting: on a weekday you may see the job being done and get a whiff of the solvents used in the lacquering process. Continue alongside the mill pond, a relic of the days when the mill took its power from a water-wheel. About half-way along on the right is the start of a drive to a house. The path to Burnslack starts a yard or two along it. It is signed but not too easy to spot. Go steeply up the field then follow the fence to find a decrepit stile. Continue along the line of electricity poles keeping above the hollow track where it drops into the clough, for the stile is not obvious and is well above the stream. From it a clear path leads through the wood to the footbridge.

Given a good day the views of the fells as you walk this length are superb. Parlick is well to the left, then comes the skyline of Fair Snape, Wolf Fell and Saddle Fell.

Head upwards towards the farm then bear left to reach its access road. Follow this to the tarmac road below Saddle End.

Saddle End to Langden Castle

Go straight across and follow the access road past Saddle End Farm and buildings onto the cart-track up Saddle Fell. After a little while you will come to a gate with the Access Area notice board. Where the track starts to rise again a little way after that gate, the track divides and re-joins in a complex fashion. Keep to the right-hand side of the fell to find a track that hugs the very edge of the valley below. It is vague to start with but becomes very well defined as a wide grassy groove and continues unbroken up the fell to the point where it makes a sharp turn to the left. (Note that it is shown as the right of way track on the OS map.) At this point take a compass bearing of around 5-10 degrees grid north. This will give you the best line across the moor avoiding the peat hags which abound in this rough tussocky ground. You will reach the skyline with its fence fairly easily and get a glimpse of Ward's Stone on the distant horizon but a view into Bleadale has to wait until you have crossed the watershed completely and started the descent. Then, keeping roughly to the same compass bearing, work your way across to the far right-hand side of the valley taking care not to lose too much height at first. The path goes further up the valley than the OS map indicates and it is worth picking it up as soon as possible for it is all rough trackless going.

Once you are on that path simply follow it down the valley enjoying the wildness and sense of remoteness. The path is reasonably well marked all the way and will bring you to the best place to cross the stream, the Bleadale Water. There is yet another stream, out of sight, to cross before you reach Langden Castle which has been beckoning for some time.

Langden Castle to Holme House

Langden Castle is no castle, but a shooting hut that offers some shelter on a poor day. The valley head rivets your attention. It is probably the finest in the whole of the Bowlands, a complex of very steep narrow cloughs. You may wonder which one you take to escape, for you may feel utterly enclosed and you will almost certainly overlook the valley of Fiendsdale on the left.

Turn left along the cart-track behind Langden Castle for a couple of hundred yards then leave it on the left at a newish signpost and follow the route marked by well spaced yellow topped poles to the confluence of Langden Brook and Fiendsdale Water. Cross the former, usually no problem, and continue up the very well marked track that is poised in a fine position above the trench of Fiendsdale. The track gives good firm going to start with but eventually reaches the peat where it flounders about in pools and peat hags to reach the fence where the Access Area notice identifies your position. Continue ahead across yet more peat to reach a badly eroded section of track. It plunges quite steeply into the great dark hollow of the head of Bleadale with Fair Snape Fell looming over you. Later the view opens up to encompass the plain of the Fylde with the tree crowned hillock of Beacon Fell to your left. When you reach the wall continue along it keeping a sharp lookout for a gate and stile on the left in about 10 minutes. Cross this and continue down the field to the rough road leading to Holme House.

Holme House to Fell Foot

Continue past the farm and go straight through the stockyard into a walled lane. Continue along this lane until it starts to swing right to go to Vicarage Farm. At this point leave it for a faint grassy track to the left that follows a hedge, becoming a full blown cart-track, very wet in places, at the gate. You simply follow it to Higher Fair

Fairsnape from Saddle End (A.Pilkington)
On Beacon Fell

In Nicky Nook
Langden Castle

Snape enjoying the fine views of Parlick straight ahead. Go through the stockyard and past the two houses then turn to have a look at them.

You will notice the upper one has a coat of arms over the door and you may be able to make out the date, 1637. The coat of arms is that of the Parkinson family and the initials are those of a Ralph Parkinson who presumably built this house. Since those days it has had many alterations. The lower house was built after the family's land had been divided following a family quarrel. It is said that the lower house was built immediately in front of the other just to spite its occupants.

Turn left through the first gate after passing the houses. Follow the cart-track until you are approaching the band of trees that lines the stream. Then leave it and go through the gate on the left and the gate almost opposite. Cross the two little streams and, facing Blindhurst, walk up the field to locate a gate and continue to a cart track. Turn right and as soon as you have crossed the stream, go steeply up the hillside to find a step stile over the fence into a rough road. A little to the left a green cart-track slants up the hillside to the right. Follow this then the line of the hedge until you reach an Access Area notice board. Cross the nearby stile, turn left along the fence to the next stile then cross the stream and contour across this large rough pasture to find the stile - a massive set of stone steps, no less, over a high wall. Drop down a little to find the stile just above the wood, and again contour to find the ladder stile. Now drop down a little to find the gate onto the lane below Fell Foot.

Fell Foot to Chipping

Turn right and cross the stile on the left in about 50 yards. The next stile lies well to the right of the gates you can see from this stile. From it bear right a little to find a gate from where you bear left then follow the hollow of the streamlet right down the field to find the stile by the gate onto the road. Turn right, keep right at the junction and immediately after it go through the farmyard at Fish House Farm. Continue along the cart-track into the field, then keep straight down it aiming just to the right of the barn, cross the little stream and the stile ahead then make straight up the field to a stone slit stile onto a farm road. Straight opposite is another stile. Now head diagonally right across the field to find the next one and then go straight ahead to the centre of the field. Now turn left and keep straight on to enter the farmyard. Turn right on the road to reach Chipping in 5 minutes.

PARLICK, FAIR SNAPE FELL, FIENDSDALE HEAD AND BLEASDALE   Walk 1.3

This is a classic short fell walk of the Chipping area with magnificent views to the west and north. The track from Fiendsdale Head drops quite dramatically into the great hollow at the head of Bleasdale and the return skirts the very foot of the fells using an assortment of field tracks.

Category:	B+
Time:	4½ hours
Distance:	8 miles
Maps:	Pathfinder Series No.668 Garstang (SD44/45). Note that this map does not cover Chipping nor the approaches to Fell Foot but it does cover the entire walk. If it is decided to start the walk from Chipping then No.669 Chipping and Clitheroe (SD64/74) will be needed as well
Start at:	Fell Foot, Chipping, which is at the very foot of Parlick. It is about 1½ miles from Chipping and can be reached from there by turning up the lane by the side of the church, keeping left at the junction ahead, left at Fish House and right in a short ½ mile. There is room to park at the sharp bend ahead or with care in the dead end lane.

Fell Foot to the High Point of Fair Snape

Walk straight up the lane to Fell Foot, not many years ago a ruin, now sensitively restored, and go through the gate on its left. You are now at the start of the brutally steep pull up to the top of Parlick Pike (1,416ft, 432m). Engage bottom gear and grind slowly upwards keeping on the left of the deep hollow. Continuing over the top of Parlick, you meet the fence of the Access Area and may cross it at several places. Do this fairly soon and follow the wall up the steepest nose of the fell then bear left to the trig point and a great pile of stones on Fair Snape Fell (1,674ft, 510m), a superb viewpoint for the Lancashire coast line given a good day.

To the north-west Morecambe Bay sits silver-blue at your feet backed by the dark mass of Black Combe whilst other Lake District hills can be made out to the right until they are cut off by the nearer Bowland Fells. Letting your eye move south the Ribble Estuary divides the Fylde from the rest of the Lancashire plain beyond which you may see the Welsh Hills, slate blue and distant. The Isle of Man? Possible, but at 70 miles away you need especially good conditions. Look just to the left of Black Combe.

A faint track takes you back to a corner of the fence (which the wall has now become). Cross it and turn left and follow it around another ¹/₂ mile, up and down numerous peak hags, until you come to a mound of stones topped with a stake that marks the highest point, 1,707ft (520m), of this Access Area.

Fair Snape to Holme House

Retrace your steps to the stile, cross over, turn right and follow the fence infallibly right the way to Fiendsdale Head, recognised in thick weather by the Access Area notices. Turn left here into a tangle of boggy peaty humps and hollows, hardly recognisable as a track but one soon appears. It plunges quite steeply into the great dark hollow of the head of Bleasdale with Fair Snape Fell looming over you. Later the view opens up to encompass the plain of the Fylde with the tree-crowned hillock of Beacon Fell to your left. When you reach the wall continue along it keeping a sharp look out for a gate and stile on the left in about 10 minutes. Cross this and continue down the field to the access track to Holme House below.

Holme House to Fell Foot

Continue past the farm and go straight through the stockyard into a walled lane. Continue along this lane until it starts to swing right to go to Vicarage Farm. Now leave it on the left for a faint grassy track that follows a hedge, becoming a full blown cart-track, very wet in places. You simply follow it straight to Higher Fair Snape enjoying the fine views of Parlick straight ahead. Go through the stockyard and past the two houses then turn to have a look at them.

You will notice the upper one has a coat of arms over the door and you may be able to make out the date, 1637. The coat of arms is that of the Parkinson family and the initials are those of a Ralph Parkinson who presumably built this house. Since those days it has had many alterations. The lower house was built after the family's land had been divided with some of their relatives following a quarrel. It is said that the lower house was built so close to the other just to spite its occupants.

Continue along the tarmac access road and turn left through the first gate. Follow the cart-track until you are approaching the band of trees that lines the stream. Then leave it and go through a gate on the left continuing through another one almost opposite. Cross the two little streams and, facing Blindhurst, walk up the field to locate a gate and continue to a cart-track. Turn right and as soon as you have crossed the stream, go steeply up the hillside to find a step stile over the fence into a rough road. A little to the left a green cart-track slants up the hillside to the right. Follow this then the line of the hedge amongst rushes. There's no clear path for some distance but eventually you will come to an Access Area fence and gate. Continue, crossing the stream in a deep cut gully where you will find a track just above the wall which takes you easily back to Fell Foot. Go through the stile and down the lane to your car.

THE FAIR SNAPE - LANGDEN CASTLE - TROUGH OF BOWLAND CIRCUIT   Walk 1.4

This grand walk could be called the classic walk of the Bowlands. It goes through some of the best scenery and given good visibility has superb views. One of the best in this book for the seasoned fell walker! It makes a circuit over Fair Snape to Langden Castle, not without some hard boggy going, goes down to the Trough road and returns by a complex network of paths hugging the foot of the fells. Most of them are not difficult to follow. Best done on a fine day in August when the heather is in bloom. The walk can be started either from Fell Foot or Chipping itself, which is a little longer, but has an easier finish.

Category:	A
Time:	7-8 hours
Distance:	15-16 miles depending where you start
Maps:	Pathfinder Series No.669 Chipping and Clitheroe, No.668 Garstang for a small portion of the walk, not essential in fair weather, and No.660 Slaidburn and Forest of Bowland (SD64/74, SD44/54 and SD65/75)
Start at:	Either Chipping car park or Fell Foot, Chipping. This is about 1½

miles from Chipping and can be reached from there by turning up the lane by the side of the church, keeping left at the junction ahead, left at Fish House and right in a short ¹/₂ mile. There is a small amount of parking space at the sharp bend ahead. It is often full on Sundays, and for that reason starting at Chipping has much to commend it.

Chipping to Fell Foot

Facing the church, leave the car park on the left and walk up the lane. Keep left at the junction, and as soon as you have passed Old Hive, turn left into the yard of Clark House farm. (This is where the camping barn is situated.) Go through the yard into the field and keep straight ahead until you are rather more than half-way across, then look to the right to locate a waymarked stile by a gate. Move across to it then go diagonally right in the next field to another waymarked stile in the corner that puts you onto the road. Go straight across it and aim to the right of the two holly trees ahead to locate the stile, then drop down left of the old barn. Cross the stile and then the stream and make straight up the field to a corner from which a cart-track leads into the yard of Fish House Farm. Turn left on the road, pass the junction and in about 50 yards go over the stile on the right. Follow the hollow on the left to a gate and continue in much the same direction to a stile. Then bear rather more to the right to find a step stile over the fence well to the left of the gate, and from there continue to the road corner just below Fell Foot.

Fell Foot to Fair Snape

Walk straight up the lane to Fell Foot, now sensitively restored, and go through the gate on its left. You are now at the start of the brutally steep pull up to the top of Parlick (1,416ft, 432m). Engage bottom gear and grind slowly upwards. Continuing over the top of Parlick, follow the fence of the Access Area to a sharp corner where you bear right and carry on for another ¹/₂ mile or so over a collection of peat hags to reach the high point of Fair Snape, a mound of stones topped with a stake that marks the true top at 1,707ft (520m) of this Access Area. You pass the stile by which the walk continues just before reaching the top.

The path towards Fiendsdale

Waymarker post at river crossing, Fiendsdale

Fair Snape to the Trough Road

The next objective is Fiendsdale Head, the top of the right of way track that runs between Bleasdale and the Trough road. Cross the fence, turn right and follow the fence infallibly through peat hags and bog pools to the right of way track at Fiendsdale Head, identified in thick weather by the Access Area notice board. Ignore other stiles.

The route more or less follows the line of the former county boundary. Before the county boundaries were rationalised in 1974 Yorkshire pushed a big salient westwards that encompassed this part of the Bowlands.

Turn right and follow the "track", a collection of peat hags and pools at first, then a good stony track poised in quite a dramatic manner above the trench of Fiendsdale. It takes you down to the confluence of Fiendsdale Water with Langden Brook which is usually easy to cross. Then follow the well waymarked track down to Langden Castle.

Langden Castle is no castle nor was it ever one, but it may feel like one if you want shelter for lunch or a brief rest on a poor day. The Castle, built as a shooting hut, is marvellously situated at the junction of Fiendsdale and Bleadale, both deeply cut valleys, and gives a feeling of being utterly enclosed in the fells.

Now follow the stony cart-track down the valley to the Trough road, bearing right at the top of the first rise. Note and deplore the many KEEP OUT notices hereabouts, but stick to your route. Thirty to forty minutes should see you on the Trough road, where with any luck you will find an ice cream cart on any fine summer's day.

The Trough Road to Higher Fence Farm

Now follow the road down the valley for a good ½ mile to the bridge that leads to Hareden Farm. Cross this and continue along the road right through this picturesque hamlet. Almost opposite the last house, a white cottage, go over the ladder stile on the left. The path is faint: climb up and to the left to find another ladder stile besides a gate. Here you find yourself on a gravel cart-track, but it is not for you. At once bear to the right and go up to the top of this long field (which runs almost to the top of Mellor Knoll), where you will find your cart-track, gate and stile in the corner. This track soon forks and you take the right-hand one which soon disappears. A yellow topped pole to the right gives you a clue as to the line to follow and another rather distant one puts you in line for the even more distant gate and ladder stile.

Never mind the bull that may be in the field, he'll be more interested in his heifers than you, at least he was when I went through. Just look around you and enjoy the widening view over the Hodder Valley. You will see that the whale back of Longridge Fell has now appeared, a cheering sign, for although you are a long way from the home straight, at least it shows you are back on the "right" side of the fells.

Now a wide but barely visible track drops gently down towards the band of broadleaved woodland that encircles the head of a great hollow of the fells. It gives superb views of the Hodder with the river making silvery curves in the lush meadows below whilst beyond the mast on Waddington Fell breaks the horizon. The path, now quite well trodden, follows the boundary wall of the wood to a little gate and continues inside the woodland for a little while. When it leaves the wood, the fire break of a conifer plantation lies straight ahead and the path continues through it, horribly wet in places, and without views of any sort. When you thankfully emerge, keep straight ahead for a few minutes to meet a tarmac lane by some hen cabins. Turn left and then right at the junction ahead to reach Higher Fence Farm just below.

Higher Fence Farm to Lickhurst

Go straight through the farmyard, cross the stream then turn left down the narrow field leaving it by a stile on the right before the end. Dinkling Green Farm is now in sight: pass to the right of the house then bear left and pass between a pair of barns onto a rough lane.

As you approach the farm you may notice that the hillocks beyond it have small limestone outcrops whilst the moors themselves are of gritstone. These hillocks are part of a series of reef knolls that extend westwards from near Grassington.

Leave the farmyard by a gate, dabble across the stream and continue along a cart-track for a short distance. Then take the left-hand fork which ends in a field. The route - for there is no path to be seen - follows the hedge round two sides of this field, to a gate in the far corner. Across the little valley lies Lickhurst Farm. Keep straight

Wolfen Hall, Saddle Fell beyond

ahead to reach the road leading to it and turn right to the farm.

The Return to Fell Foot

Go past the house and where the track swings to the left go through a gate on the right. This is the start of the so-called Stanley Road. It is not shown on the map as a right of way but is well used by walkers. It is not a road in the accepted sense but a pleasant, often green, cart-track that will take you to the lane just below Burnslack. Avoid two right-hand forks that go down to the stream, and at a sweeping left-hand bend where the track temporarily disappears, keep by the side of a deep cut groove until the track reappears. Cross the ford - sometimes tricky - and continue past the ruins of High Barn to the lane.

Turn left and continue for almost a mile along this delightful lane fringed with hawthorn in spring and glowing rowan berries in autumn. Turn up the access road to Saddle End Farm and just before you reach the house turn left by a telegraph pole to find a stile that puts you on the top side of the fence. Turn left and follow the path through the trees. After the first stile continue to follow the fence to a gate and stile then go straight into the deep cut tree filled valley that separates you from Wolfen Hall. A rather shaky footbridge takes you over the stream and a good track leads to a gate. Change sides of the fence at another stile and continue past the barn to reach Wolfen Hall and go left onto the farm access road, which brings you onto the road where you are parked.

The Return to Chipping

As you reach the farm turn left into the "road" between the farm buildings and continue along it to the end of the buildings on the right-hand side. There you will see two gates side by side: go through the left-hand one aiming a little to the left of the trees crowning the rather distant hill. In due course you should reach a broad shallow trench running the length of the field, possibly a relic of the former Leagram deer park. Follow the trench to the fence and you will find the stile on its left. Now head up the field well to the left of the obvious gate to locate the stile which is hidden from view behind a dip in the ground. A prominent horse-chestnut tree may help you to find it. Turn left through the gate and continue along the access road to Park Stile, lined with trees in a way that suggests Park Stile was once a house of some importance. Immediately beyond the house and buildings, at the point where the lane becomes green and has hedges, turn left through a gate. Go through two fields bearing slightly right to find the bridge across the stream hidden in the belt of trees, then aim for the junction of fence and wall to find the stile. Now go straight ahead to the right of Chipping Lawn to join a tarmac lane and follow this down to the road where a right turn and 10 minutes sees you in Chipping.

OTHER WALKS

CHIPPING TO BURNSLACK, returning by LICKHURST
Walk 1.5

An afternoon's walk of variety and considerable quality, reaching the edge of the fells and returning through the fine park land of Leagram Park. An alternative shorter return is given that avoids the stream crossings.

Category:	B or C
Time:	about 3 hours, 2 for the shorter walk
Distance:	6 miles, 4½ for the shorter walk
Map:	Pathfinder Series No.669 Chipping and Clitheroe (SD64/74)
Start at:	the car park, Chipping.

This walk uses the same start as Walks 1.1 and 1.2 which it follows as far as the gate out of the farmyard at Saddle End. Here there is a signpost to Burnslack and you simply follow the cart-track to the right. After some 15 minutes it slides off into a field on the right whilst the right of way track is now the rush filled ditch on the left. It reverts to a good cart-track in less than 50 yards and Burnslack Farm, cradled in a great hollow of the fells, comes into sight almost at once. Continue towards the farm, pass in front of it, and carry on down their access road, enjoying good views of Longridge Fell. Where this track curves to the right and becomes tarmac, turn left on the fell road to Lickhurst or cross the stile almost opposite if you are using the short return.* This is a rough winding cart-track, wet in places and with a ford that can be troublesome in wet weather, but there is more than one place to cross besides the ford itself. It has good views towards Pendle Hill, too.

At Lickhurst go past the house then turn right between the buildings. At the very end of this long farmyard, a gate opens into a hawthorn shaded lane that wanders pleasantly along in the direction of Knot Hill Quarry. The lane eventually opens into a large field crossing a tiny stream on the way, and continues as a cart-track to the right. You, however, leave it and head up the field to a gate in the top corner, which very soon comes into view. Once through this, simply follow the fence on the right through four fields to Knot Hill quarry, long disused.

Knot Hill is one of the series of reef knolls that are to be found on this side of the River Hodder. See the geological notes for more about reef knolls.

Once in the field where the quarry hillock is, bear right past the end of it then head towards the left-hand one of two pieces of woodland.

The boundary of the Leagram Deer Park is thought to have been down the side of this wood. The remains of the bank can be seen, very much smaller than it would have been.

You'll find a stile into the woodland about 50 yards to the left. Go straight down the hillside till you reach the level bit then turn sharp left to find the new bridge. It's a delightful spot, with firm, well drained grass in the curve of the stream, and sheltered. Just the place for a break. Now climb steeply up the opposite bank and simply follow the fence/hedge on the right, crossing a tiny stream on the way, to reach the farm access road to Chipping Lawn in front of a clump of conifers. Now simply turn left, following it to the road through fields graced with stately trees. Now turn right and 10 minutes along the road sees you into Chipping.

The Short Return*

Having crossed the stile opposite, head diagonally right to find the stile in the corner by the gate and continue in the same direction to the next corner and gate. Now simply follow the wall then the hedge to Windy Hill Farm. Pass the barn on the left, turn right between the barn and the house and as soon as you are through the gate, turn sharp left to drop down to the footbridge and your outward route, which you retrace to Chipping.

ALONG THE FOOT OF THE ACCESS AREA   Walk 1.6

This walk uses a collection of green tracks and farm roads, most of them used on other walks, that run along the foot of the fells. It takes the walker into the great hollows at their foot, passes the Bleasdale Circle and has some of the ambience of the higher ground, as well as passing some of the interesting houses of Bleasdale. It will suit the walker who likes the ambience of the fells but who dislikes the heavy peat going. Not that this walk is free from boggy bits or stream crossings! It can be split into two parts at Fell Foot, using the finish of Walk 1.1 or the Start of Walk 1.4.

Category:	B+
Time:	5 hours
Distance:	11 miles
Maps:	Pathfinder Series No.669 Chipping and Clitheroe and No.668 Garstang (SD64/74 and SD44/54)
Start at:	the car park, Chipping. It is well signed and has toilets.

Chipping to Blindhurst

Facing the church, turn left up the lane, and keep left at the road junction. In a couple of minutes you will come to a lane on the left with a public footpath sign. Follow this lane to its end, cross the stile and head diagonally right to find a stile about half-way along the hedge. Continue in the same direction passing the corner of the wood to find the stile more or less opposite. Climb steadily up the field to the top right-hand corner where you do a right and a left turn round the corner of the field, then follow the hedge to enter a short length of lane leading to Cold Coates Farm.

You may notice a trig point on top of this lowly hillock as you pass. Turn round, and you have a wonderful panorama before you. On the right is Longridge Fell. If you ever wondered how it got its name, now you know. Further left is the Big End of Pendle Hill, the Chatburn cement works throwing polluting plumes into the air on a still day. Then comes Waddington Fell identified by its mast, and to the left the entire skyline of the Bowland Fells from Parlick to Saddle Fell is stretched out. Chipping lies below, easily spotted by its church tower. No wonder there is a trig point here.

Turn right on the lane and right at the T-junction ahead. Almost at once turn left just past the house following tractor marks up the field to a stile in the left-hand corner. Then follow the line of the hedge and stream to Woodgates, a well built house, built by a member of the Parkinson family in 1768, with a difficult-to-read Latin inscription over the door. Turn right on the road and after 50 yards or so turn left into the access road to the yard of Hill Crest. Almost at once climb the banking on the left to find a stile into the field, then follow the hedge up the field to a fine staircase, no less, over the wall. Now head for the low side of the barn at Higher Core, go straight across the farm access road through a very narrow gate and follow a wall/fence/wall/fence sequence down the field to locate a good footbridge. Then head towards the only bit of wall in the hedgerow ahead to another stone stile and cut across the field to reach the access road below Blindhurst.

Follow the track through the little hamlet, and have a look at the principal building, painted quite strikingly black and white, though not in keeping with the architecture of the house.

It has mullioned and transomed windows but a fine Georgian doorway partly hidden by a crude wall no doubt built to keep the farm livestock away. The datestone above the door suggests the reason for this blend of architectural styles - 1731, a time of transition when long low mullioned windows were going out and the pillared Georgian doorways coming in. Note the garage at one end, formerly probably a stable. It is a common feature in most of the houses passed on this walk. The house was built by Richard Edward Parkinson in 1731 whose initials appear on the datestone.

Blindhurst to Holme House

The preliminaries are now over. Ahead lies Bleasdale Fell, seen for the first time. Bear left through the farmyard onto a good cart-track. At the end of the first field go through the left-hand one of two gates and continue until the track peters out. Then aim at a little hen cabin at the end of a belt of trees and ford the stream. At some time or other there was a concrete bridge here and its remains may help you to cross. Now follow the fence on your right to the access road to Lower Fair Snape, turn left, and leave it for a gate at the first bend about 100 yards away. Go straight across the field aiming for the centre of the wood and cross the right-hand one of two stiles. Continue straight ahead to the road, a few yards short of the crossroads where the village school is situated. Turn right, pass the school and soon after you will come to the parish church of St Eadmer.

Though solid and plain, it is always open, an oasis of peace and quiet on a day when the wind and rain are roaring outside. There has been a chapel on this site since Stuart times, if not before. It was rebuilt in 1835, when the name St Eadmer, who was a contemporary of St Anselm, Archbishop of Canterbury was given to it. The names of early Christian saints were often given to rebuilt churches in Victorian times.

Beyond the church the tarmac continues for a little way passing Vicarage Farm. You may notice the words "Bleasdale Circle" on the map a little way to the east of the farm. There is no public access to it but it's worth asking for permission to visit at the farm. It is reached by turning into the fields on the right just after crossing the cattle grid and is in the clump of trees.

Bleasdale Circle is no ordinary stone circle, indeed, it has been called a "Woodhenge", for its posts were of wood, not stone. The site is a flattened circular mound about 35ft in diameter and surrounded by a wide shallow ditch. Eleven short concrete pillars now mark the sites of the original oak posts that formed the circle and six more form a short avenue facing east. The site was first noticed in 1898 when there were no trees round it and thoroughly excavated in 1898/9 and again in 1933/5 when the original oak posts were replaced with short concrete pillars. In the centre of the mound at a depth of about 2ft a stone lined cist or chest was found which contained two cremation urns one of which held a smaller one. Both were full of broken, charred bones. The whole was surrounded by a palisade of oak poles to give a circle about 180ft in diameter within which a number of burnt circular patches of earth each some 3-4 metres in diameter were found. It is thought that these burnt patches were the sites of huts that had been destroyed by fire, and that the inner circle had been a burial area. A radio carbon date of 1890- 1810 BC was obtained from timber taken from the inner circle. Assuming this to be correct, and it is confirmed by the design of the collared urns, the Bleasdale Circle is the site of an early Bronze Age village, a rarity indeed.

Continue along the road to the point where it swings left into Admarsh Barn Farm and there take the grassy cart track to the right. *There are excellent views of the fells ahead, culminating with a look into the great hollow - it would be a cwm if it were in Wales - between Fair Snape Fell and Bleasdale Fell before you turn your back on it abruptly.* The track leads to Holme House, but when you reach the part where there is a wall on its left, keep a lookout for a faint green track on the right. It follows the hedge and becomes well marked at the first gate. You simply follow this cart-track, very wet in places, straight to Higher Fair Snape enjoying the fine views of Parlick ahead. Go through the stockyard and past both houses then turn to have a look at them.

You will notice the upper one has a coat of arms over the door and you may be able to make out the date, 1637. The coat of arms is that of the Parkinson family and the initials are those of a Ralph Parkinson who presumably built this house. Since those days it has had many alterations. The lower house was built after the family's land had been divided following a quarrel. It is said that the lower house was built close to the other just to spite its occupants.

Continue along the tarmac access road and turn left through the first gate. Follow the cart-track until you are approaching the band of trees that lines the stream. Then leave it and go through a gate on the left continuing through another one almost opposite. Cross the

Higher Fair Snape, Bleasdale with Fair Snape Fell behind

two little streams and, facing Blindhurst, walk up the field to locate a gate and continue to a cart-track. Turn right and as soon as you have crossed the stream, go steeply up the hillside to find a step stile over the fence into a rough road. A little to the left a green cart-track slants up the hillside to the right. Follow this, then the line of the hedge amongst rushes. There's no clear path for some distance but when you reach the Access Area notice board, cross the nearby stile, turn left along the fence to the next stile then cross the stream and contour across this large rough pasture to find the stile - a massive set of stone steps, no less, over a high wall. Drop down a little to find the stile just above the wood, and again contour to find the ladder stile. Now drop down a little to find the gate onto the lane below Fell Foot.

Fell Foot to Chipping via Burnslack

Almost opposite is the access road to Wolfen Hall. Follow it past the house, a rather undistinguished building despite its name and history, and turn right before the barn. Turn left at its end, right as soon as you have crossed the stile, go through a gate and down a good cart-track to locate a wobbly footbridge in the tree filled valley. Various little tracks lead you up the hillside opposite into a wet pasture. Keep to the left to find the stile and keep left again to pass above the belt of trees, only dropping down through it at the last minute to reach Saddle End's access road.

Turn left on it and go straight ahead to the gate out of the farmyard. Here there is a signpost to Burnslack and you simply follow the cart-track to the right. After some 15 minutes it slides off into a field on the right whilst the right of way track is now the rush filled ditch on the left. It reverts to a good cart-track in less than 50 yards and Burnslack Farm, cradled in a great hollow of the fells, comes into sight almost at once. Continue towards the farm, pass in front of it, and carry on down their access road, enjoying good views of Longridge Fell. Where this track curves to the right and becomes tarmac, there is a stile into the field across the road. Head diagonally right to find the stile in the corner by the gate and continue in the same direction to the next corner and gate. Now simply follow the wall then the hedge to Windy Hill Farm. Turn right between the barn and the house and then turn sharp left to the footbridge. Go up the field to the stile on the right and follow the line of poles across the field, then drop down to find the stile onto the road just above the furniture works. Ten minutes down it sees you in Chipping.

THE RIVER BROCK AND BLEASDALE   Walk 1.7

This walk starts by following the River Brock upstream for almost a couple of miles to one of the many minor roads in the area, passes Bleasdale Tower and uses a collection of farm access roads and field paths to return to the River Brock some way downstream of the car park.

Category: B
Time: about 5 hours. Route finding is not difficult.
Distance: 11 miles
Map: Pathfinder Series No.668 Garstang (SD44/54)
Start at: the car park at Higher Brock Bridge, which is used for the Brock Valley Nature Trail and has a delightful riverside picnic area. It is easily found from the A6. Leave it at Claughton Lane Bridge which is

$^{1}/_{2}$ mile south of the junction of the A6 with the B6430 that runs through Garstang and is easily identified by a garage on the corner. It is signed Beacon Fell. After crossing the M6 turn right at the T-junction and left after a good $^{1}/_{2}$ mile. Follow this wriggling road for a couple of miles to another T-junction then turn right to find the car park by the river in $^{1}/_{2}$ mile.

Higher Brock Bridge to Weaver's Farm

Cross the bridge and immediately turn left into the gateway besides Brock Farm Cottage. The site of Lower Brock Corn Mill was somewhere hereabouts. Follow the cart-track into a large field, turn right and follow the fence, then continue in the same direction to a stile next to a white painted gate. This puts you on a path right on the very edge of the river bank and which you follow through the woods for 10-15 minutes.

The woods are a delight in early May. The air is heavy with the scent of hawthorn and bluebells, the grass full of flowers. You will see the gaunt stalks of butterbur, long since finished flowering, red campion, water avens, stitchwort, comfrey here and there, and foxgloves getting ready to add to the later woodland display. Almost every common plant of the Lancashire countryside is to be found in season: you may even spot the well named orange tip butterfly or other less easily identified ones.

As you approach a set of large pipes crossing the river bear right through the gorse bushes to the top of the embankment. Head towards the cottage and just beyond it, slightly left into the wood. A well used path continues along its foot, muddy in parts with a few ups and downs, and you will reach a footbridge in 10-15 minutes. The right of way now turns right up the track, Snape Lane, that leads to it, but it is quite practicable to continue up the valley. The track is vague at first, but shortly it becomes a deep cut stony track. Follow this up the hill for a short $^{1}/_{2}$ mile to the tarmac road and at the end of the wood turn left down a bridleway into the wood. There used to be a finger post "Bridleway to Brickworks Woods" here. It may be replaced some day. Follow this track right down into the woods. When you reach the level ground the path becomes vague but head towards the river.

If you look to the left in the middle of this glade in the woods you will see, in the middle distance, a small fenced enclosure. In it there is a memorial stone to Cyril Spiby, a well known rambler and guidebook writer, and a specially planted oak tree.

Near the river bear right and a well marked path quickly develops. Continue upstream passing through what looks like a youngsters' adventure playground with a path and steps up the hillside. It is part of the Waddicar camp-site for Lancashire Scouts and Cubs. Beyond it the valley is more open and the scenery splendidly park-like with stately trees. Carry on to a new footbridge, cross it and continue up the valley leaving it by a well trodden path that starts in the gorse bushes and climbs up the hillside to reach the road almost opposite Weaver's Farm.

Weaver's Farm to Delph Lane

Turn into the farmyard sparing a glance for the initials W.G. and the date, 1847, set in white pebbles in the side wall. (For their significance see the note about Bleasdale at the end of this walk.) Continue through the farmyard onto the tractor track and follow it through the field to the road where you turn left and continue along it to the road junction at Brooks Barn.

On a good day the road gives fine views of the fells from Parlick to Bleasdale and allows you to inspect the ancient packhorse bridge at Brooks. It's a tiny structure compared with those of the South Pennines, but has the characteristic low parapets of pack horse bridges.

Turn left at this junction and continue along the road.

It does not give very interesting walking but it passes through varied scenery - at first woodland where you may catch a glimpse of the grey squirrel and hear the metallic honk-honk of the pheasant, and later open pasture with views to Beacon Fell. The buildings scattered along the road have the look of Victorian estate architecture, for part of Bleasdale belonged to W.J.Garnett, a mid nineteenth-century philanthropist who lived at Bleasdale Tower, which is tucked away in the trees on the left.

Soon after passing it there is a lodge on the right and further on still, Fell End Farm. Just beyond the road becomes rough and unmetalled again. At this point leave it and make for a little wooden gate in the band of trees ahead, it gives a useful short cut to the road, Delph Lane, where you turn left.

Delph Lane to Higher Brock Bridge

Almost at once turn right through the second of two gates that are opposite a narrow but clean cut gap in the trees. The start of the track is extremely muddy but it rapidly improves and leads you to Higher Landskill Farm. (Keep your eye on the posse of collie dogs - especially the quiet one.) At Landskill, a name of Norse origin, turn left into a grassy hedged lane between the first farm building and Higher Landskill Farm. In the field follow the hedge side on the left for quite a distance, passing a brick/stone/concrete platform to reach an awkward gate on the left. Continue up the field to reach Cobble Hey. Go straight ahead onto the farm's access road and follow it to Infield House where you bear left in front of the first building, re-built in 1991. Continue to the piggeries at Butt Hill and bear right to reach the public road. Not great walking this, but easy, and having a good view of Sullom Hill, another Norse name, across the River Calder.

Turn left on the road and opposite the entrance to Butt Hill turn right over a stile into the fields. There's no path to follow now, simply set off diagonally left and keep to the right of the electricity poles following them to Foggs Farm. Make for the gate well to the left of the farm buildings and again go just to the right of the poles to find the footbridge over a deepish ditch. Yet again be guided by the poles to find the exit stile from this field, then turn right and follow the edge of the field to the gate onto the road.

Go straight across and up the field aiming for the roofed gap between the buildings of High House Farm, whose dwelling has mullion windows. Note that there are plans to change the right of way path, so keep a lookout for signs. Continue ahead and a little to the left to a hedged lane that ends shortly in the fields. Go diagonally left over the crown of the hill, not through the gate, to locate the stile. Then turn left and follow the fence through two fields, leaving the second one through the left-hand one of two gates. A short length of grassy lane takes you onto the road at Clarkson's farm, now semi-ruined.

It's a rare example of a building that was thatched with rushes, a style once fairly common on the Fylde plain, but rare in the Bowlands. The steep pitch of the roof and the deep barge boards are the tell-tales and the rushes can be seen in the cowshed roof, tacked on to the kitchen.

Turn right on the road and turn left after a couple of minutes to follow a road down to Walmsley Bridge where you turn left onto the riverside, arguably the finest stretch of the River Brock. There's only a trace of a path through the water meadows and stretches of woodland until you reach a wide track coming down the hillside on the left which originally lead to Brock Mill. You have now joined the River Brock Nature Trail, and you simply follow it upstream to the car park. After a minute or two Brock Mill is signed to the right. Divert if you want to have a look. See walk 1.8 for something about the mill and the natural history of the trail.

About the Parish of Bleasdale

There never was a village of Bleasdale, though this widely scattered community still supports a church, a village school and a post office. In the early years of the nineteenth century a certain amount of industry was established using the waterpower of the River Brock, one of the parish boundaries. Apart from those mills already mentioned there was a cotton mill almost opposite the present post office cum cafe which was then a blacksmith's shop. Much of Bleasdale's nineteenth-century history is tied up with the work of W.J.Garnett, whose father, W.Garnett, a merchant of Liverpool and Quernmore, bought Bleasdale Tower, then a simple building, to use as a shooting lodge in 1831. It was enlarged in 1847 and became the home of his son, W.J.Garnett, who was MP for Lancaster from 1857 to 1864 and became a well known agricultural reformer and philanthropist. He owned a large part of Bleasdale, most of it poor wet land which he improved by draining using the newly invented round clay drain pipes, even setting up his own factory to make them, using clay found locally. He organised the drain laying and charged his tenants for it, unusual in those times. They were then able to apply fertilisers to improve crop yields and keep better breeds of cattle and sheep. As a philanthropist W.G.Garnett was somewhat unusual, setting up the North Lancashire Reformatory School at Bleasdale in 1857. He built Clough Head Cottages to house the occupants with the aid of a government grant, but made good the inevitable shortfall out of his own pocket. Reform schools were then a new development in the handling of juvenile offenders, aiming to reform rather than punish. A maximum of 125 youths from various Lancashire towns were housed in the cottages and were found work on the land and taught various trades such as stone masonry and shoemaking as well as the common agricultural skills. *They received some general education on the wet days, and the school remained open until 1905. A monument to its occupants' skill and effort remains, for they built Clough Head Bridge, not passed on this walk but on walk 2.5. The church and Bleasdale circle are visited on Walk 1.6.*

THE BROCK VALLEY NATURE TRAIL
Walk 1.8

The Brock Valley Nature Trail lies about a mile due west of Beacon Fell and can easily be combined with a visit there. Unlike Beacon Fell it is easily found from the A6. Leave it at Claughton Lane Bridge which is ¹/₂ mile south of the junction of the A6 with the B6430 that runs through Garstang and is easily identified by a garage on the corner. It is signed Beacon Fell. After crossing the M6 turn right at the T-junction and left after a good ¹/₂ mile. Follow this wriggling road for 2 miles to another T-junction then turn right to find the car park by the river in ¹/₂ mile.

To find the car park from Beacon Fell, leave the circular road by the exit on the north-west corner: it is signed to Preston. Turn left at the first junction and again at the second, then take the first right. The car park is a good ¹/₂ mile down this road at the second bridge.

Category:	C
Time:	about an hour
Distance:	1¹/₂-2 miles
Maps:	none needed
Start at:	the car park at Higher Brock Bridge a very pleasant spot with a picnic site.

The Trail

Leaflets describing the nature trail are available from The Development Officer, Lancashire Trust for Nature Conservation, The Pavilion, Cuerden Valley Park, Bamber Bridge, Preston, PR5 6AX. It has to be said, however, that in spring of 1990 not a single post marking the stations is left, though new footpath signs are in place. This in no way spoils the enjoyment of a first rate riverside path, at its best in late May. Simply follow the river downstream as far as the ruins of Brock Bottom Mill then retrace your steps. The right of way path does in fact continue to the A6, but this is not part of the nature trail and is outside the Forest of Bowland. The path divides and rejoins many times but all footpaths leaving the nature trail have "public footpath" types of signs. The land belongs to Claughton Hall Estate and is leased to Wyre Borough Council who manage the trail jointly with the Lancashire Trust for Nature Conservation. The fishing is private.

Things to Look Out For

The River Brock is fast flowing in times of heavy rain and has carved miniature cliffs in the glacial deposits of its banks. There is one of these soon after leaving the car park and the erosive powers of the river in flood are very obvious by the collapse of the path a little further on. Here the rounded stones washed out of the boulder clay form a bed below the cliff and a number of different types can be easily seen.

There is a good selection of typical woodland plants in May in the varied habitats. In different places according to the needs of the plant, you will find bluebells in quantity, wild garlic, red campion, clover, butterburr, greater stitchwort, water avens, herb bennet, sweet cicely, comfrey, yellow iris, and no doubt, others. Later in the summer you will find meadow sweet, rosebay willow herb, and that invasive foreigner, Himalayan balsam.

Some distance downstream you will pass a large chunk of concrete work in the river bed, the remains of a weir that diverted some of the river water to the mill pond which supplied the water-wheel that powered Brock Bottom Mill. A little further you may come to a footbridge (this is where comfrey grows) and just beyond it there is a large terrace where two rows of mill workers cottages once stood. The ruins of Brock Bottom Mill itself are shrouded by trees and scarcely visible in high summer. However, a finger post directs you to them but a fence and locked gate prevents a close inspection, perhaps as well, they look distinctly unsafe. It is possible to gain some idea of the buildings from the fence but hardly practicable to make a circuit - they are too close to the river. The mill was considerably larger than it appears at first sight and its water-wheel was fed by two ponds, one of them immediately above the mill and onto whose embankment you may climb the better to see its size.

When you have had your fill, retrace your steps to the car park.

About Brock Bottom Mill

It is known that there was a paper mill at Brock Bottom in 1786 but it was demolished about 1790 when a James Lorimer, a wealthy merchant of Preston, built a new cotton spinning mill. The Industrial Revolution was progressing rapidly, Arkwright's waterframe had been invented twenty years previously and there was money to be made in cotton spinning. The new mill had twenty frames, and was complete with a joiner's and a blacksmith's shops, twenty cottages for the mill workers and their families and a stable. The mill thrived in its early years but soon the competition from less remote mills, and later from big steam driven mills in nearby Preston became severe, and by 1851 the mill was having problems. It was badly damaged by fire sometime in 1860 and that was the end of it as a spinning mill.

However, it was rebuilt in 1861 as a roller-making factory (rollers were used in the spinning mills) and carried on until 1891 when it started to make files. During this time the mill took its power from a water-wheel, but a heavy flood in the 1930s badly damaged the weir. Repairs were not satisfactory so a gas engine was bought, but the money lost as a result caused the business to close in 1936. A little community continued to live there: it had its attractions despite its remoteness and the primitive state of the houses, for they were very small and had neither electricity nor running water, people taking their water from the river. The cottages were condemned in 1945 but a few people continued to live there until 1951.

BEACON FELL COUNTRY PARK

BEACON FELL   **Walk 1.9**

Beacon Fell is a little knob of tree girt moorland on the very edge of the Lancashire plain. It has been a Country Park since 1970 and has seen considerable development for the benefit of visitors. A narrow one-way road encircles it in a clockwise direction and on it there are five fairly small car parks, the one at Fell Foot having a picnic area and toilets. All except one, the Quarry car park, are quite close together on the south facing side of the Fell. The sixth one, Carwags, is not on the "ring road", but about 1/2 mile to the south-east and is marked on both the 1:25,000 (sheet 668) and 1:50,000 (sheet 102) maps. It has toilets, a picnic area and an information centre with a display about Beacon Fell, though it is open only on summer weekends. A pleasant path connects it to the path that encircles the eastern side of the Park and links all the car parks. This path is well made and easily identified as it is surfaced with wood chippings, or pitched with stone. There are a number of other paths, some well prepared, others rough and muddy. The Park is extremely popular, rightly so, for it offers easy walking in a variety of environments from thick silent forest to open fell with superb views, and requires neither boots nor special clothing. It follows that it offers neither peace and quiet nor solitude.

Finding Beacon Fell

Beacon Fell is one of the trickiest places in the whole of the Bowlands to find as it is embedded deep in a mesh of lanes. The 1:50,000 map sheet 102 is extremely useful in case of mistakes. It is signed from many places but most signs disappear when you need them most and you may find yourself doing a grand tour of the Lancashire countryside and ending up where you started. However, the signs from Inglewhite seem to be continuous and bring you to the car park above Crumbleholme Fold. Though small this is very close to the larger one at Fell Foot. To find Inglewhite from the M6, leave it at junction 32, take the A6 to Broughton, a short mile, then the B5269 to Goosnargh. Now turn left at the sign to Inglewhite and Beacon Fell. Carwags is probably most easily found by doing the circuit of the Park from Cumbleholme and leaving it at a sharp corner on the left. It is then about 1/2 mile down the road on the left.

The Circular Path and the Summit of Beacon Fell

Category: C
Time: an hour, more or less
Distance: about 2 miles
Maps: none needed, but it is marked on Pathfinder Series No.668
             Garstang (SD44/54). The sketch map should make things clear.
Start at: for preference either Fell Foot or the Quarry car park. If you are
             obliged to park at either of the others on the south side, turn left
             along the road to Fell Foot, which is quite close. If you are at
             Carwags then follow the path up the hill and cross the road to reach
             the circuit path and turn right. It will take about 10 minutes.

If you have parked in Fell Foot start the circular path by the notice board. It takes you over a shoulder of the forest and down to the road. As it starts to drop turn left to continue the circular track. Avoid the stony forestry road. Now follow it right round to the northern side passing the Quarry car park where you will come onto the open fell with its excellent view of Parlick and Fair Snape Fell.

If you have parked at the Quarry leave by the notice-boards turning right to join the circuit path. The track then turns left up the hillside to reach the trig point. The brass plate on top of the pillar enables you to identify distant places and gives the distance to each place. It was presented by the Ramblers Association to mark European Conservation Year in 1970 but unfortunately most of the places it shows to the south have been blotted out by trees since then. However, to the north-west, Blackpool Tower is 17 miles away and often visible; the Isle of Man is 78 miles distant and can only be seen if the atmosphere is extremely clear and usually at sunset when the island is a dark silhouette against a bright sky. Others such as the power station at Fleetwood have been demolished. To continue the circuit a wide but poor track in the rough grass of the fell follows the side of the wood to the road. This has good views to the north and west. Turn left on the road and follow it back to Fell Foot car park, taking care with traffic.

Beacon Fell Summit Direct from Fell Foot Car Park

Start up the cobbled path by the notice-board and when it levels out turn left at the crossroads of paths. Bear left at the fork and a few minutes sees you there. Either return as you came or complete the circuit path.

Hay baling, Bowland

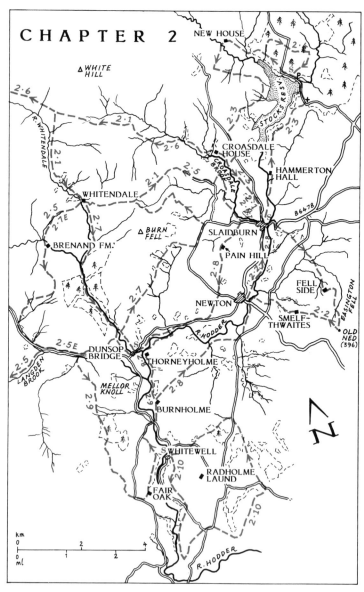

NEW HOUSE

△ WHITE
HILL

STOCKS RESV.

2·6

R. WHITENDALE

2·1

2·6

2·3

2·3

CROASDALE
HOUSE

HAMMERTON
HALL

2·5

BROADSDALE BROOK

B6478

WHITENDALE

2·1

2·5

2·7

2·1

SLAIDBURN

2·8

△ BURN
FELL

PAIN HILL

2·5
2·7E

BRENAND FM.

FELL
SIDE

2·2

EASINGTON FELL

2·8

NEWTON

SMELF-
THWAITES

2·2

2·7

OLD
NED
(396)

2·5E

DUNSOP
BRIDGE

THORNEYHOLME

R. HODDER

2·5

LANGDEN
BROOK

MELLOR
KNOLL

2·8

2·9

BURNHOLME

N

WHITEWELL

2·10

RADHOLME
LAUND

FAIR
OAK

2·10

2·10

R. HODDER

km
0   2   4
0   1   2
ml

Chapter 2

WALKS ROUND SLAIDBURN, DUNSOP BRIDGE AND WHITEWELL

About Slaidburn

Starting at Slaidburn
2.1 Croasdale and Whitendale, Category A
2.2 Easington Fell, Category B
2.3 A Circuit of Stocks Reservoir, Category B
2.4 Forest Walks at Stocks Reservoir, Category B
2.5 Slaidburn to Garstang over the fells, Category A+
2.6 Slaidburn to Wray by the Hornby Road, Category A

Starting at Dunsop Bridge
2.7 Dunsop Bridge - Dunsop Head - Whitendale Circuit, Category A or B
2.8 Walking the Hodder to Slaidburn, Category B
2.9 Above the Hodder Valley, Category B

Starting at Whitewell
2.10 Through the Radholme Deer Park, Category B

ABOUT SLAIDBURN

As you approach Slaidburn by the road from Dunsop Bridge, St Andrews Church makes an immediate impression, being poised on higher ground above an ancient flight of steps. A second look dispels the first one as the exterior walls are all cement skimmed - and that does nothing for any building - and its rather small windows are square headed and plain. Its tower is quite massive, doubly buttressed and having slits from which arrows could be fired, a reminder that Scots raiders were active in the North of England in the early years of the fourteenth century, particularly after Bannockburn. There are beam holes on either side of all the doors, a clear indication that the church was a stronghold for the villagers in those troubled times.

61

The great merit of the church is its interior, little changed since the eighteenth century. There's a wealth of box pews, each designed to hold an entire family in cosy privacy, many of them having dates on the door, the oldest 1616, the newest 1749. Some of them bear the names of the families or farms on neat brass plates. There's one for Smelfthwaites (Walk 2.2), one for J.Bleazard of the remote House of Croasdale (Walk 2.1). Box pews like this were the reason for the building of three decker pulpits in many churches, and as one might expect, Slaidburn's church has a fine example installed in 1740. Much earlier than this is the rood screen, a fine piece of Jacobean work, and the screens that enclose the two chapels are even earlier, probably early fifteenth century. Another piece of ancient woodwork is the font cover whilst the font itself is a very plain Norman one.

Next to the church is Brennand's Endowed School, a fine but simple Georgian building. It was founded and endowed by one John Brennand who, as the lintel stone tells us, lived at Pale Hill, a farm about a mile from the village, and who died in 1717. It is still the village school, and its modern extensions are tucked away round the back out of sight from the road.

As you walk into the village the Hark to Bounty, the village pub, lies straight ahead. Its name arises from the days when deer hunting with dogs was still a pursuit of the gentry, and a visiting squire or parson, so the story goes, hearing the hounds baying outside, exclaimed, "Hark to Bounty", his own favourite hound. The name stuck, far more distinctive than the original Dog Inn. The building must have been one of some importance in earlier years, for the Halmote Court was held there in an upper room which still retains its original oak benches, dock, and witness box. The Halmote Court was the chief court of the manor where all types of offences such as failure to work the required number of days for the lord of the manor, or illegal hunting, or wood cutting in the forest were tried. Slaidburn was head of the manor of Grindleton at the time of the de Lacy family's occupation of Clitheroe castle. There are a number of houses with date stones of the seventeenth century: earlier ones rarely survive, nor has Slaidburn's other pub, which is now a simple though very well used youth hostel.

Possibly of greater interest in these times is a car park with toilets. It is on the Settle road close to the river, a very pleasant spot.

Hark to Bounty, Slaidburn

STARTING AT SLAIDBURN

CROASDALE AND WHITENDALE FROM SLAIDBURN
Walk 2.1

Croasdale Brook is a major tributary of the Hodder which it joins in Slaidburn. This walk joins the brook and follows it for over a mile to reach the Hornby Fell Road leaving that after a good 2 miles to drop into the head of Whitendale. It then crosses the fells a second time in order to return to Slaidburn. As usual there are no trodden paths to follow out of Slaidburn but after the third stile the route goes in a remarkably straight line to Shay House. The prime time for the walk is early autumn when the heather is in bloom.

Category:	A
Time:	6-7 hours
Distance:	12½ miles
Map:	Pathfinder Series no. 660 Slaidburn and forest of Bowland (SD65/75)
Start at:	The car park, Slaidburn. This is on the Settle road close to the river and has toilets. Refreshments are available in a number of places in the village.

Slaidburn to Croasdale House

Turn right on leaving the car park and wander through the village to the War Memorial, a bronze statue of a Tommy raised on a column. The parish lost many men in the Great War. Turn right here, cross the bridge over Croasdale Brook and go up the hill for about 70-80 yards when you will see a footpath sign to Croasdale on the left. Then go diagonally right up the hillside towards the group of trees. Follow a line of trees, the remains of the field boundary shown on the OS map, into the wood keeping left of the end of the wall. The step stile is in the dark corner. From it go slightly left to see the stile ahead then go straight through three large fields, hayfields in early summer. You will find yourself above Croasdale Brook winding its way down the valley and not a stile in sight. Make for the loop of the stream at the end of the fence to find it and continue in the same direction through two more fields to a cart-track that leads to Shay House.

There are fine views of the fells as you go through these fields and you may wonder which of the valleys you will walk up. When Shay House comes into view all is clear enough. It is the valley slightly to its left winding entrancingly into the fold of the hills ahead.

Go straight across the cart-track and cut the loop of the river to find the stile. You will shortly pick up a wide gravel track which you follow to Croasdale House, a lonely but well kept farm sheltered from the winds by its sycamore trees.

Croasdale House to Whitendale

Go through the gate to the left of the farm and almost at once cross the little stream on the left. Follow the cart-track up into the field where, after the manner of its breed, it ends abruptly. Work your way along this vast flat topped field to the right and keep a look out for a bridge below. Drop down to it when it comes into view, cross it and continue through the gate onto a thready track that contours the rough grasses of the hillside a little way above the brook until the ruined House of Croasdale is in view. What little there is of it now disappears from view and leaves you to make your way up to the ruins by the best line you can find. Here there is a modicum of shelter on a poor day for lunch - provided the nettles are not too tall. There are no other sheltering walls until you are well down

The gorge, Whitendale
The hamlet of Whitendale

Browsholme Hall
Riverside cottages at Slaidburn

Whitendale.

Go through the gate beyond the ruins onto a pleasant green cart-track that slants up the hill to the fell road beyond. You now follow this road, roughly metalled in places, for the next 35 to 45 minutes to a gate in a fence.

It's hardly first-class walking but allows you to enjoy the view of Croasdale Brook and as Great and Little Bull Stones on the fell above draw near you will know the road has not far to go.

Beyond the gate all traces of hardcore and concrete disappear and the road becomes a peaty morass in places if the weather is wet. Continue for another 10 minutes until the road starts to rise slightly and becomes grassy. Then look for a post down the hillside to the left. This and subsequent posts mark the line of the right of way track from the fell road into Whitendale. There's no track at present, just work your way from post to post. They are widely spaced but will take you down to the brook near a quite elegant cairn and a well defined track. Now simply follow this track down the valley to the gate in the wall above the tiny hamlet of Whitendale, about 30 minutes of very agreeable walking. Having gone through the first gate bear right to a post to pick up a cart-track that will lead you to the hamlet.

The scene changes quite quickly as you come down the last part of the valley. The rather bleak stream running down from the moors enters green sheep dotted fields sheltered by woodland. There is no sign of the well kept houses for they only come into view at the very last moment.

Whitendale to Slaidburn

Now the hard work really starts! It is not as bad as it looks because the track up the fellside has an easy gradient. Turn left at the house, and go past the farm buildings to the fell gate where the track starts. Follow its zigzags up the breast of the fell to a sort of turning circle on the right of which a well trodden track continues through the heather right to the gate in the wall at Dunsop Head.

A yellow topped pole marks the start of the track and could be useful but the needless succession of them that follow are an annoyance, distracting from the sense of remoteness and isolation that are an essential part of the pleasure of moorland walking. You might be glad of one or two more just beyond that gate, but after the manner of so many waymarks, there isn't one just when you would be glad of it.

At the gate that track instantly and completely disappears and there is a choice of route according to the OS map. The one to the right gives pleasant grassy walking once you have crossed the initial band of very wet ground, then a mile or more of road walking. The one to the left is a much rougher track towards the end but has much less road to deal with and this one is described here. At the gate look slightly left and find a yellow topped post across an expanse of boggy ground, not easy to see in poor light. Go across to it on the faint track. The next one is almost invisible but is planted in an area of stony ground slightly to the right. Again a faint path leads to it. Now you should be at the start of a pleasant green cart-track that crosses the moor and finally drops quite steeply down to the start of a fell road at a sharp corner where there is a gate.

There are some excellent views as you cross the wide watershed of Dunsop Head. First of all the Big End of Pendle comes into sight slightly to the right. Then a little later when you have crossed the boggy moor - no time for viewing then - Pen-y-Ghent comes into view crouching like a lion viewing the flat topped Fountains Fell as if it were its dinner. By degrees it sinks from view as you loose height but is replaced as a focal point in the scene by Stocks Reservoir. Even that disappears when you reach the road, just when you need a diversion, though Easington and Waddington Fells now come into sight.

Go down the road, quite pleasant relaxed walking without traffic, and good views, for a short mile. When you come to the first right-handed curve after Higher Wood House, just beyond an isolated barn turn left into a grassy lane. It is quite short and at its end a stile brings you into the fields. Climb fairly steeply up the centre of the field and when you are opposite a wide gate with stile by it in the left-hand wall, you are also opposite the stile in the right-hand fence, not nearly so easily spotted, but the one you want. Continue down the field, pass to the right of the barn and to the right of the house to join its access road. Turn right and as soon as you have crossed the bridge turn left over a stile. Make for the little gate between the buildings ahead, Myttons. Go straight across the yard into a walled lane and where it ends keep left following the wall. Go through the gateway ahead and bear right to find a footbridge, a massive slab of rock, and a stile. Turn left and follow the fence by the

Looking up Croasdale

stream, our old friend Croasdale Brook, and then when that makes a wide loop to the left, continue straight on until you meet it again in the woods ahead. Now follow the well used path to the road, turn left and in a few minutes you pass the Hark to Bounty, useful if the time of day be right. Straight on at the crossroads sees you at the car park.

EASINGTON FELL FROM SLAIDBURN   Walk 2.2

Easington and Waddington Fells are the two highest points (1,299ft (396m) and 1,296ft (395m) respectively) on the fells that separate the Hodder from the Ribble. Strangely, Easington Fell is not named on the Pathfinder map though it is named on the 1:50,000 Landranger map. The TV mast that serves the area is situated on Waddington Fell making it easy to identify and Easington Fell lies on the other side of the Clitheroe-Newton road. This walk offers fell walking free from peat bog, very pleasant pasture and a riverside path, whilst the descent gives excellent views of the southern part of the Bowland fells.

Category: B
Time: 3½-4 hours
Distance: 5 miles
Maps: Pathfinder Series No.660 Slaidburn and Forest of Bowland and
              No.669 Chipping and Clitheroe (SD64/74 and SD65/75)
Start at: Slaidburn car park

Slaidburn to Fell Side and Old Ned

Cross the river bridge and climb up the steep road to the first gate on the right beyond the sharp bend. Walk up the field towards the trees then bear left towards the corner to find the stile by a gate. Continue along the wall side changing sides at a gate to reach the road and go straight across it to Broadhead Farm. Cross the stream, turn right into the field and go diagonally left to the gate. Continue up two fields towards Skelshaw, now in view, crossing a sizeable stream at the top of the second one to reach the farm. Pass through the top of the stockyard and go across the back of the house to join the access road leading to Fell Side, about ½ mile up the fell. Here go straight ahead through the gate and turn left onto the open fell by a wide rough cart-track. Follow this along the fell for about ¼ mile until it splits into several parts, then take the lower one which winds round into the valley behind the fell immediately above the house, for this is Sadler Fell, not Easington Fell. It disappears in a while but keep straight on to pick it up again as a very narrow track just above a bracken patch. Work up the hillside a little and you will find it becomes a full blown cart-track again, crossing from the right- to the left-hand side of the valley at its apparent head. Now simply follow it to Old Ned, a dumpy cairn of biggish stones. Another similar cairn about 250 yards away to the left is known as The Wife.

Old Ned to the Top of Easington Fell and Back

The true top of Easington Fell is now only a short mile away and it seems a pity not to visit it, for given a good day it is a superb view point.

From the cairn the whole of the Bowlands Fells that face south extends before you. Stocks Reservoir is easily picked up glinting in the sunshine. Slaidburn is well to its left, further left still a great wide V gap locates the

Trough road and Dunsop Bridge. Behind to the left is the rounded end of Totridge Fell and then, not so easily distinguished, are the trio of Saddle, Wolf and Fair Snape Fells with Parlick a modest bump at the end. Beacon Fell can just be made out on the edge of the lower Ribble valley, then the eye leaps round to rest on the massive ridge of Pendle Hill. No mistaking the dominant hill of Ribblesdale, and forget it not, an outlier of the Forest of Bowland Area of Outstanding Natural Beauty. An undistinguished mass of low hills follows, then Embsay Moor and Fountains Fell lead the eye to Pen-y-Ghent and Ingleborough, the circuit well nigh complete.

BUT there is no right of way to the summit. It's your own affair if you indulge in a spot of trespassing!

Retrace your steps to Old Ned.

Old Ned to Newton

First line up Old Ned and his Wife then turn your back on them. This gives you the line to take down the trackless moor to find a faint track in the rough grass. It strengthens rapidly and becomes an overgrown cart-track cutting across the moor between Brown Hill and Sadler Fell, passing a small tarn to your left before you arrive at the steep edge of the fell.

From here the view which has tantalised you as you picked your way across the moor is suddenly revealed in all its splendour. Dunsop Bridge at the mouth of the Trough road is away to your left, fairly easily identified, and from it a complex array of fells and moor spreads eastwards. Behind the Trough road a flat topped fell stands well above the rest. This is Ward's Stone, at 1,836ft (561m) the highest point in the Bowlands.

The rough track zigzags down it - take care to turn right at the last zig to reach the correct gate. Go down the rushy field to a very difficult gate at Smelfthwaites Farm, bear left through the farmyard onto their access road and turn into the first gateway on the right. Now the character of the walk changes and goes through lush green fields, typical of the park-like countryside in this corner of the Bowlands. Go down this long field to Meanley keeping to the left of a shallow tree filled gully. At the bottom of the field bear right to the gate, then cut between the outbuildings and the house to reach the access road. Follow this down to the tarmac, turn left, and after about 150 yards go through a gate on the right onto a wide cart-track leading into a long field. Walk its full length to a stile by the gate and follow the curve of the river to a stile onto the bridge at Newton, comfortably in view.

Newton to Slaidburn

Cross the bridge and immediately turn right onto a well trodden path by the River Hodder lazing along in deep dark pools. Go through the stile on the right in the field ahead and follow the fence through this long riverside field to a gate at the foot of the steep wooded hillside. Now follow a path or cart-track along its base to emerge on the road at a pair of ornate iron gates, relics of departed grandeur. Slaidburn lies about ¹/₂ mile ahead. Bear right in the village centre to find the riverside car park.

A CIRCUIT OF STOCKS RESERVOIR   Walk 2.3

This walk makes a gentle tour round the reservoir which is visually much more interesting than most and not obscured by gloomy conifers nearly as much as the OS map suggests. It has many bays and inlets, even an island and the walk gives exceptionally good and varied views. Because there is no path across the dam nor path across the valley between there and Slaidburn, the walk starts at that village. It goes along the length of the east side of the reservoir partly through Gisburn Forest then crosses the Hodder at a ford and returns on the western side, only a field's breadth from the water in places, by a quite remarkable and easy footpath.

Category:	B, for though quite long, there are no steep hills to climb and it is all easy going without route finding problems.
Time:	about 5 hours
Distance:	9 miles
Map:	Pathfinder Series No.660 Slaidburn and Forest of Bowland (SD65/75)
Start at:	Slaidburn car park or equally well from Gisburn Forest car park on the banks of the reservoir which is reached from the Settle road out of Slaidburn. This starting point has the advantage that Slaidburn offers refreshments and toilets at rather more than the half-way point, but the walk gives a more satisfying change in the landscape when done from Slaidburn.

From Slaidburn to Gisburn Forest Car Park

Turn right on leaving the car park, continue to the War Memorial and turn right there. As soon as you have crossed the bridge over the River Croasdale turn right into the fields. Cut across to the rather distant wall corner, then follow it to a wide gravel road. Turn right here crossing the River Hodder where you may see trout in the deep pool below the bridge and follow the road to Hammerton Hall.

Hammerton Hall was once a fine Elizabethan house, three storeys high, even with a three storey porch, built on the traditional E plan with the porch forming the short bar of the E. It has square headed mullion windows except on the ground floor where unfortunately they have been replaced with larger modern ones. No less unfortunately quite a number of the upper ones have been blocked up and modern chimneys spoil the roof line. That said, it is still a very fine house, of a size, age, and calibre not common in the Bowlands, though common on Pendleside. The strange three storey porch is a status symbol and the women of the household would use its well lighted middle storey for spinning and needlework. As the name suggests, it once belonged to the Hammerton family, but they lost all their lands and property following the part they played in the Pilgrimage of Grace in 1536. (This was an armed protest in the North of England against the closure of

Hammerton Hall, one of Slaidburn's historic houses

St James' Church, Stocks Reservoir

the lesser monasteries. It was ruthlessly put down and those participating were beheaded and had their lands and property confiscated.) The present hall was built by one Oliver Breres and embodies parts of the Hammerton's house.

Continue to the farm buildings and take the right-hand fork. You will see three gates almost side by side. Go through the left-hand one where a welcome yellow waymark has been fastened, and you will find waymarkers on almost every stile until you reach the road corner at St James' Church. Go straight up the field following the wall then continue with the wall on the other side to reach a stile into a rough lane edged by forestry on the left. Stocks Reservoir lies below you on the left, out of sight.

In due course you will come to a length of woodland that has been cleared and get your first view of the reservoir. The embankment lies well to the left with Board House in a commanding position above it.

Follow the lane until it ends at a field stile (note that the right of way path enters the field earlier than the OS map indicates) and continue in the field in the same direction. It will bring you to a gate above Black House. Go past the house on the left and follow their access road to the tarmac road at a corner by isolated St James Church.

Knowing nothing about the area you would wonder whatever a church was doing there. Inside the church, mounted on the wall, you will find a note about its history and a faded newspaper cutting that gives a fairly full account of life as it was in the village of Stocks in Bolland or Dale Head ,as the village was often called in the days before World War II, and its submersion in the reservoir.

The village was situated between the island - which you will see as you walk along the road - and the "mainland" and had about 20 cottages, a shop, post office, a school, and a pub, the Travellers Rest. Its church, built in 1852, stood a little distance from the village on what is today the Gisburn Forest car park. When the Fylde Water Board built the dam in 1922 to contain the waters of the River Hodder to assuage the thirst of Blackpool, the church was pulled down and rebuilt on its present site and a little later the graves were exhumed and reburied there. What of the village itself? As was commonly done in those days before the chemical purification of water the villagers were moved from their homes and the houses demolished. The villages of other valleys inundated by reservoirs suffered a similar fate. Think of Mardale, now below Haweswater, Lady Bower below the Derwent Reservoir in the Peak District, Watergrove near Rochdale. The outlying farms not affected by the reservoir building have been bought up by the Forestry Commission as they came onto the market and the afforested area is slowly increasing.

Continue along the road to the Gisburn Forest car park, about a mile. You can shorten the last bit by using part of the forest trails that start from the car park. When you have passed the start of a forest road look out for a gap in the hedge and a marker pole topped with a red and a blue ring. The path makes a small diversion and brings you back to the road further on. Then you cross the road and continue by path to the car park. Worth it if the road is busy. You will have a good view of the reservoir from time to time but there is no access to its shore at any point.

The road is far from dreary, for it does not run between ranks of gloomy conifers and its verges are very colourful in late summer and early autumn. There are rows of giant fox gloves, willow herb, purple knapweed, meadowsweet in the wetter places all backed up by glowing orange rowan trees. You will hear ducks and the honking of Canada geese on the reservoir in autumn and winter, possibly see them in flight wheeling over the water. You may see some quite rare birds in winter for the reservoir offers many different habitats. In springtime black headed gulls nest on the island filling the air with their raucous cries.

Gisburn Forest Car Park to the "Railway" Path

Go through the car park onto the waymarked bridleway beyond. Three trails start here, two of them marked by poles topped with a red and a white ring and these are your guideline along the bridleway. After 10 minutes or so you will find one with a yellow arrow pointing to the right, for this is where these two forest trails go, but you keep straight on. In a couple of minutes you will come to a clearing with a stone shed. Take the left-hand fork here and you will emerge from the forest at a gate in a few more minutes, no doubt pleased to have wide open views again, for you look right up the Hodder to the fells.

Go straight ahead from the gate following a very faint green cart-track that bends to the right to find a stone bridge over Hasgill Beck. The track is now very plain and takes you to the ruin of New House, once quite a little hamlet, in about $^1/_2$ mile. When you are within about 50 yards of the ruin turn left through a gateway and you find yourself in a few yards on a walled lane, once the hamlet's "street". Turn left and in about another 50 yards go right through a gate into the field. Turn right and follow the wall to a gate. From this gate a wide green track leads you down to the ford across the Hodder. The river is wide and stony and presents no problem - save the risk of going over the boot tops - in normal weather. If however, you don't like the look of it, it takes but a few minutes to retrace your steps to the gate by the barn and follow the wet weather alternative.

Assuming you cross, hopefully still dry-shod, go across the field to the obvious gate which lets you in to the ruined hamlet of Collyholme, which sits astride a tiny stream covered with stone slabs no doubt for safety. Go left through a large gap in the wall then go up the field fairly close to the stream to locate the stiles. The first is utterly ruinous but the second is in good order. Bear left a little and shortly you will be on a wide green track making for the gate in the corner.*

The Wet Weather Alternative

Continue past the barn on the cart-track (not shown on the OS map) that goes through a large field to Catlow. You however, leave it before Catlow, at the head of Parks Clough, a deep cut stream bed filled with trees. Go down the right-hand side of this by a grassy track to the road below, unfortunately tarmac. Turn left and follow it past Kenibus to the Slaidburn-Bentham road. Turn left on the road and follow it to a sharp corner with a barn on the left, a short $1/2$ mile. Go through the gate onto a good gravelled cart-track and follow it through two fields. You join the main route in the second field. Continue to the gate in the corner.*

A few yards beyond the gate you leave this enticing track and bear right through an unpromising area of rushes. On the other side you can see a good green track and you continue along this excellent wide track, very obviously built up above the level of the surrounding land. Shortly you will see what looks very much like a railway cutting, which is exactly what it is, for you are walking along the line of a narrow gauge railway built to bring stone from a quarry just off the Bentham-Slaidburn road to the Stocks Reservoir when it was built in the 1920s. Follow the old track for a good $1^{1}/2$ miles, reassured from time to time by posts with a yellow waymarker arrow. You leave this remarkable track where it starts to swing round a big hollow at a point marked by an orthodox footpath sign.

Climb steadily up the hillside fairly close to the wood passing a ruined barn then aiming fair and square at the next one. Again well spaced posts give some guidance. Continue straight up behind the ruins, cross a hollow that is the start of a little stream and you will pick up a well trodden little path. This path takes you over the spur of the hill to the next stream which you cross on a single flag bridge then bear left to the far corner of the wood. Over the stile the path disappears for a time. Keep going bearing slightly to the left and strain your eyes for the next marker post. Once found go straight down the field to pick up the cart-track leading to Hollins House at a gate. Turn right and in 10 minutes you are on the road.

Turn left on the road and follow it down the hill for around 10 minutes to the start of the track to Shay House and Croasdale. Turn right here, though if you prefer, you can stay on the road right into Slaidburn; quicker, but not so agreeable. As you approach the river turn left over a stile into the field. Continue straight across it to find the stile, similarly in the next one where the stile is in the bottom corner. Now go slightly left up the hill following the line of a row of hawthorn trees and when they end, keep in the same direction through this long field to find the stile. Go through two more long fields keeping in the same direction and as you are approaching the wood, make for the corner. Once over the massive stone step stile follow the line of trees, the remains of an old hedge, into the field, and take a slanting line down to the stile onto the road. Turn right and very shortly you are crossing the bridge where you started.

FOREST WALKS AT STOCKS RESERVOIR   Walk 2.4

There are three quite short waymarked walks in the Gisburn Forest at Stocks Reservoir, the longest only taking 75 minutes, the shorter pair 50 and 45 minutes respectively. These two are merely shorter variants of the long one which is waymarked in red, whilst these are in white and blue respectively. See the sketch diagram. The Gisburn Forest is far more open than the map suggests with large unplanted areas, others scattered with self sown young birch trees. Views from the topmost forest road are particularly good.

Category: B, because of the wet rough going at the start
Time: as above
Maps: none needed, simply follow the waymarks
Start at: Gisburn Forest car park, best reached from Slaidburn by crossing the river bridge and following that road for almost 3 miles to a crossroads where it is signed on the left. The car park is at reservoir level and easily missed, for it is tucked away in the forest where the road makes a right-angled bend to go uphill again.

The red route is probably the finest of all and it is best to start by continuing from the car park through the thick forest, close to the shores of the reservoir. A bold well sited post shows you where to leave this track and you climb steadily up a rough and often wet track for a considerable distance to the forest road above. Here you turn left and follow this road for a mile or more through very open forest with fine views extending from Pendle, to Waddington Fell to Tottridge Fell, all of them embracing the reservoir below. You'll pass a picnic table then come to the public road. Go straight across this, continue on easy, level going to the point where it swings left. Here, in the corner on the right, is the white waymarker directing you to the shorter route back if that is your wish, whilst yours acquires a blue ring, for this is where the blue route joins the red. Gradually the road drops down the side of a valley with a stream below and curls round and delivers you to the tarmac road not far from the car park. Turn right, take not more than a couple of strides and turn right into the wood to follow a pleasant little path that keeps you off the road and gives you good views of the reservoir as a bonus. The white and blue routes join you just before you reach the car park.

SLAIDBURN TO GARSTANG OVER THE FELLS   Walk 2.5

This is one of *the* classic fell walks of the Bowlands. It takes a good direct line, first crossing Dunsop Head to reach Whitendale, then goes neatly over to Brennand Farm. From there it makes a sizeable climb up the fell behind the house then descends to the Trough road at Trough Barn. Next it goes up the valley of the well-named Langden Brook, continues up Fiendsdale, crosses over into Bleasdale and finally reaches Garstang by a collection of farm access roads and field paths. Almost all of this ground is covered in walks 1.4, 1.2, and 1.7 in that order, though some portions are reversed. See these walks if you are interested in what is to be seen as you gallop through.

This walk was very popular with walking clubs from the Bolton/ Manchester area in the early 1950s. In those days people went to Clitheroe on the train on Saturday, walked to Slaidburn over Easington Fell, stayed the night at the youth hostel, and returned home from Garstang by bus. Similar tactics are once again possible with the re-opening of the Ribble Valley Rail link. Trains every hour connect with the local bus services. For timetables ring the Clitheroe Tourist Office 01200 25566. If you have a traffic manager, he/she should park in the big free car park in the centre of Garstang, infallibly reached if he/she arrives by the B6430 from the south.

Category:	A+, for it is 20 miles and has 2,500 feet of ascent, and plenty of peat bog. Route finding is easy even from Bleasdale to Garstang.
Time:	9 hours for a fairly strong walker
Maps:	Pathfinder Series No.660 Slaidburn and Forest of Bowland, and No.668 Garstang (SD65/75 and SD44/54)
Start at:	The youth hostel or car park in Slaidburn

Slaidburn to Dunsop Head

From the youth hostel go past the Hark to Bounty and continue along the road that goes to Newton by the foot of the fells. If you are using the car park return to the village to locate this road. Continue up it until just beyond the health centre there is a path on the right signed to Woodhouse. Follow this well trodden path through the wood and along Croasdale Beck cutting across a loop to follow it a little further. Then, after a stile, cross a slab bridge over a side stream and continue straight up the field to the corner. Again follow the wall to enter a short length of walled lane that brings you to Myttons, now a craft centre. Bear left in the yard to find a stone slit stile beyond the craft shop from where you head diagonally right to the corner of the field. Turn right and go through a gate immediately before the buildings and head for the barn. Then follow the hedge/fence through two fields. In the third, as you approach the spot where the spot height 191 is marked on the map, turn left and follow the hollow green track to a short lane and the road. Turn right and follow it for about a mile to the fell gate. Just beyond this, leave the Hornby Road which you are now on, and take the track over the fell which climbs steeply up on the left. As it levels out at the top of its climb it virtually disappears leaving you to follow a set of widely spaced yellow ringed poles to reach the little gate at Dunsop Head. For this reason, in thick weather you may prefer the alternative route which involves a good deal more road walking.

Alternative Route to Dunsop Head

Start as above but keep on the road beyond the health centre for almost 1^{1}/$_{2}$ miles, then when you have gone round a well defined left-hand bend turn right into the newly tarmacked track that leads to Burn Side Cottage. Keep right at the cottage through a gate marked with a blue arrow and continue through the goat's pen to another waymarked gate then into a vast field that runs up to the base of the fell. Keep near the wall to start with and when you see a stake on the left cross the wet hollow to find a narrow path on a raised ridge of good grass. It will lead you right up this rough wet field to the fell gate at the top.

A deep cut hollow track now leads to the right, makes a sharp turn left and continues up the fell right to Dunsop Head. Where the track splits take the left-hand one which curves round to the head of the valley but as you approach the wall at Dunsop Head the track disappears in a wet green morass. Deal with this as best you can and keep on to the gate, which is further than you think.

Dunsop Head to the Trough Road

From the gate a well trodden peaty track marked with an unnecessary number of yellow topped poles leads you down to the end of the shooting track above Whitendale Farm. Follow this cart-track down to the farm and the road. Turn right on it and 20-30yds brings you to a stout wooden bridge from which you go over the shoulder of the fell to Brennand Farm.

There's scarcely any path to be seen but eventually a path appears leading you to a small gate in a wall. Through this turn left for about 100 yards then bear right to one of the many yellow topped stakes on this route. The path now passes through a big area of rushes, very wet indeed. Many pathlets go through it trying to avoid the worst...take your pick and make for the corner of the fence ahead.

Lead mining was carried on hereabouts in the mid nineteenth century and the pond and mine spoil heaps you pass are a result of it.

Carry on to the stile and then down the field to the corner where big spoil heaps can be seen the other side of the wall. Pass between the big spoil heaps to find the cart-track and gate. The cart-track continues and a little way along a branch goes off to the right. Follow this right down to Brennand Farm. Turn right in the farmyard passing the house into the fields beyond. Go through two gates in quick succession then bear right whilst climbing quite steeply to find a winding rushy hollow. Follow it right up this long field to a pair of stiles. From them the path is quite distinct if narrow, winding its way to the left and to the Ouster Rake track up the fellside. The path continues to a wire fence and stile, but before reaching it spare a moment for the views behind which are very fine.

You are now considerably higher than Middle Knoll, a grassy green hill separating the two valley heads and well seen against the darker heather of Dunsop Head. Beyond the green fields to its left on the far horizon is Wolf Hole Crag, identified by two tiny needles quite a long way apart.

After the fence the path becomes very faint and the line of stakes is quite a help. On the steepest part bear right to find a ladder stile over the wall. The path is still faint: aim for the bracken patch ahead and as you approach the walls around the ruins of Trough House you will find a stony cart-track. Simply follow this to the Trough road, almost a mile away. Here turn left and freewheel down the road for a short mile to a stand of larch trees on the right, where on most summer days you will find a refreshment van - ice cream, burgers, drinks hot and cold.

The Trough Road to Bleasdale

The path to Bleasdale starts in the trees as a metalled road leading to the waterworks house. Beyond the house it becomes a pleasant cart-track leading to Langden Castle. Take care to keep on the lower track all the time. Langden Castle is no castle, but a shooting hut that offers some shelter on a poor day. Continue along the cart-track for 200 yards but leave it on the left at a newish signpost and follow the route marked by well spaced yellow topped poles to the confluence of Langden Brook and Fiendsdale Water. Cross the former, usually no problem, and continue up the very well marked track that is poised in a fine position above the trench of Fiendsdale. The track is good firm going to start with but eventually reaches the peat where it flounders about in pools and peat hags to reach the fence where the Access Area notice identifies your position. Continue ahead across yet more peat then a badly eroded section of track which becomes pleasantly green takes you to the intake wall above Holme House. Follow it for about 10 minutes to a stile built into a gate then go down the field to reach the access road to the house.

Holme House to Calder Vale

Turn right along the rough road and follow it for 2 miles to Delph lane. The road becomes metalled at Hazelhurst, and remains a mixture of tarmac and concrete until it joins the public road. Though this does not give very interesting walking it passes through very varied scenery - first woodland where you may catch a glimpse of the grey squirrel and hear the metallic honk-honk of the pheasant, then open pastures with views to the rounded dome of Beacon Fell. The buildings you pass have the stamp of Victorian estate architecture, for this is precisely what they are. First you cross

Typical Bowlands! Near Langden Castle

Clough Head Bridge, then you come to Clough Head Cottages and at the next house, Brooks Barn, you turn right. Bleasdale Tower (See Walk 1.7 for an account of W.J.Garnett's walk there) screened by trees is some little distance, though soon afterwards there is a lodge on the right and further on still, you come to Fell Farm. Just beyond the farm the road becomes rough and unmetalled again. Now comes the point of this catalogue, for here you leave the road and make for a little wooden gate in the band of trees ahead. It gives a useful short cut to the road. Turn left, and after a few minutes turn right through the second of two gates that are opposite a narrow but clean-cut gap in the trees. At the start the track is extremely muddy but it rapidly improves and leads you to Higher Landskill Farm. (Keep your eye on the posse of collie dogs - especially the quiet one.) Go straight through the farmyard and follow this concrete access road's zigzag course down to Calder Vale. When you are above the end of the mill (1) keep a look out for a set of steps on the left. They cut the corner of the road quite neatly. You then pass the Methodist chapel where the toilets are open to the public on Saturdays and Sundays until 8pm. Across the bridge the post office sells such things as ice cream and sweets.

Calder Vale to Garstang

Continue up the road pondering which route to take for there is a choice from Calder Vale to Heald Farm. You may turn right up a steep flight of steps just past the end of Victoria Terrace or you may continue along the road until it meets Strickens Lane. Despite the greater amount of road this route's continuation across the field to Heald Farm is far pleasanter underfoot than the other which is a churned muddy tractor route once you've crossed the road. At the junction with Strickens Lane the stile is directly opposite. Make towards the left-hand corner of the field to the gate, keep on to the next gate and the one after that. Then turn right and follow the hedge to the farm. Here swing left to find a little gate by the side of the building that lets you into a cattle yard and from which you emerge on to the farm's access road. If you prefer the steps, from their top you enter a narrow hedged footpath that passes through a wood and leads you into a field. Go straight across it and the next one, then cross a footbridge and shortly bear right to reach the road.

Turn right and in a mere 20 yards or so turn left across a stile and join the muddy tractor track mentioned above. It takes you to the back of Heald Farm where you look out for a stile on the right into a bit of open woodland. Follow the path through that to the farm access road where you turn right.

However you have arrived at this point, Garstang (2) is now in full view and less than an hour away. Continue down the farm access road and go straight across the junction below, pass Clarkson's Farm and carry on to Parkhead Farm. (Note. This short length of road is not shown on the 1:25,000 map, but it is shown on the 1:50,000 map sheet 103.) Go past the farm, over the motorway bridge and into the field on the left by a concrete stile. Bear diagonally left aiming for Greenhalgh Castle Farm, easily identified by the remains of the castle (3), cross a deep cutting and turn right when you reach the tractor route. Go through the farmyard and continue along the road to the road bridge over the River Wyre. Turn right, bear right at the roundabout, passing a handy cafe, and continue for less than 5 minutes to the bus stop. If you want to find the car park, continue past the market cross to the shops in Market Street and go through the ginnel just beyond the King's Arms. The car park with toilets is directly opposite.

Things of Note Passed as You Dash Along

(1)   Calder Vale is a mill village and the mill, a cotton weaving mill was still operative in 1992, a rarity. It was built in 1835 by two brothers, Richard and Johnathan Jackson, who were Quakers. It was a combined spinning/weaving mill, with spinning on the top floors and weaving on the ground floor as was customary, and was originally water-powered. The leat can still be seen at the end of the houses where the farm access road makes a hairpin bend. Today its looms are powered by electricity and they run 24 hours a day, 7 days a week. The chimney serves the boiler used to raise the steam used to create the humid atmosphere needed for cotton weaving. The village was built as a model village at the same time as the mill and had a temperance hotel with a reading room, but naturally, no pub.

(2)   Garstang does not lie within the boundaries of the Forest of Bowland but merits a word or two. It is an ancient market town, centre for the cattle trade in the days when vaccaries flourished in

the Forest of Bolland. It stands upon the historic line of the A6 as it was in the 1930s, on the Lancaster Canal, and on the former London Midland and Scottish railway whose branch to the docks at Fleetwood left the main line at Garstang. The importance of all these communication systems greatly diminished in postwar years so Garstang has regained its identity as a quiet market town, still with its market cross and has become a place of considerable character.

(3)   Greenhalgh Castle was built by the 1st Earl of Derby in 1490 as a fortified house, castles as such being rather out of date by that time. He made an extremely good job of it as in the Civil War 150 years later the 7th Earl of Derby's garrison held out so long that it was one of the two last strongholds in Lancashire to fall to the Parliamentarian forces. The Earl himself was captured soon after the Battle of Wigan Lane and beheaded at Bolton in 1651.

SLAIDBURN TO WRAY BY THE HORNBY ROAD   Walk 2.6

The other of the two classic crossings of the Bowlands and considerably shorter and much easier than its companion, the Slaidburn to Garstang walk. The Hornby Road is probably a former packhorse route between Slaidburn and Hornby and uses the line of the Roman road from just above House of Croasdale to the high point where the Roman road bears right to go down into the head of Hindburndale. From High Salter there are options:

1) the road to Wray which is tedious and only to be given serious consideration in failing light.

2) via Haylot and Thornbush, scenic but longer and with considerable re-ascent. If you choose this option you will need Pathfinder map No.637 Burton-in-Kendal & Caton as well. It is fully described in Walk 4.6.

3) via Harterbeck and Outhwaite is the shortest route and is free from route finding problems once Harterbeck is reached.

A transport manager is probably essential - or an exchange of cars. The journey by the gated road over the moor from Bentham to Slaidburn is quite direct and not too long. There is no car park in Wray and it is probably best to leave a car at Meal Bank Bridge on the Bentham road where there is room to park at the picnic place.

Category:	A
Time:	6-7 hours
Distance:	14 miles, 16 miles via option 2
Maps:	No.650 High Bentham and Clapham and No.660 Slaidburn and Forest of Bowland (SD66/76 and SD65/75)
Start at:	the car park, Slaidburn

Slaidburn to High Salter

The walk uses the same start as Walk 2.1 following it until it leaves the Hornby Road just before the high point. This walk then continues along the Road to High Salter, a distance of about 7 miles.

The road is marked "Roman Road" on the map but it is variously concrete, churned up peat bog and good grass, no sign of Roman work at all except at the high point where it can be seen swinging away from the grassy road and going down the nose of the fell into the head of Hindburndale.

High Salter to Wray via Harterbeck

Go through the gate opposite the farmhouse and go straight ahead down the field to a stone step stile near the corner. Now cut diagonally right across this large field to a gate and then head towards the wall to find the stile in the corner. Again cross the field diagonally to the right dropping down steeply as you approach the wall to find the bridge at the head of Pedder Ghyll. Follow the green track to Harterbeck, cross the road and go through the gate opposite then through the first gate on the left. Continue down the field and after the next gate join a stony cart-track where you turn right and follow it to the end at the barn. Keep going in the same direction until you see a slit stile and head for it. Again continue in the same direction crossing a rushy field to pick up the line of a totally collapsed wall on your right. Follow this to a gate where the route now keeps alongside the wall for almost a mile to enter a short length of green lane close to Outhwaite. Cross this hamlet's access road to the stile and walk down two long fields to find a little stone slit stile partly masked by a holly bush. Cross it and turn right to reach the road a good mile above Wray. Freewheel down to Wray, cross the bridge and immediately turn right to take the riverside path back to Mel Bank Bridge.

About Wray

Wray and the Roeburndale valley suffered severe damage in the flood of 1967 caused by a cloudburst over the fells that put down some 8″ of rain in a few hours. The whole of the valley was flooded; bridges and houses were swept away, even Meal Bank Bridge. The Memorial Gardens by Wray Bridge were made on the site of cottages swept away or damaged beyond repair in the flood, though the bridge itself stood firm. The great damage in the village was caused mainly by trees blocking this bridge and allowing the water to build up until it burst out sweeping all before it.

Wray was a prosperous village by the early seventeenth century judged by the dates on several houses. Records of the Quaker community there show that the community was well established by the middle of that century and had its own meeting room and graveyard by 1703. It is now the Methodist school room. Wray had a silk weaving mill in the nineteenth century, now known as Bobbin Mill, as for a time bobbins were made there using locally cut timber. The last silk hat made there is displayed in Lancaster Museum.

The converted bobbin mill, Wray

STARTING AT DUNSOP BRIDGE

DUNSOP BRIDGE - DUNSOP HEAD - WHITENDALE CIRCUIT   Walk 2.7

This walk takes little used field paths across the foot of Beatrix Fell to the start of the track that leaves Back Lane, Slaidburn, to go over Dunsop Head to Whitendale. Most of the route over the fell is on a good track and though the return from Whitendale down the valley is on tarmacked road it is not without its merits. From Whitendale the walk can be easily extended to Brennand Farm and virtually the same return made down Whitendale, indeed it can be extended yet again to reach the Trough road. If you intend doing this, it is better to park at the entrance to Langden Brook on the Trough road in order to split the rather long length of road walking into two parts. It is a walk with great variety of scene, best done on a clear autumn day when the bracken is tawny brown and the trees golden, contrasting with the green grass of the pastures.

Category: B, A if the extension to the Trough Road is done
Time: about 4 hours. Add on a short hour if you do the extension to Brennand Farm, 2 hours if you extend to the Trough road.
Distance: 9, 10½, or 13 miles respectively
Map: Pathfinder Series No.660 Slaidburn and Forest of Bowland (SD65/75)
Start at: Dunsop Bridge car park. This is at the Slaidburn end of the village.

Dunsop Bridge Start

Turn right on leaving the car park and go along the road to the metalled bridleway immediately beyond the post office. Follow this for about 10 minutes to a row of cottages at the mouth of Whitendale. Go past them and over a stile at the left of two small gates beyond the outbuildings. About half-way between the stile and the footbridge ahead look out for a broken down stile* on the right, easily missed.

Trough Road Start

Walk down the unfenced road for a good mile taking great care with the traffic. After passing the road to Hareden keep a good lookout for a finger-post on the left by a gate, perhaps ½ a mile away. From

Beatrix Farm, Staple Oak Fell behind

it a bridleway, unmarked on the ground, cuts across to the tarmac road that runs up to Whitendale. Turn left on the road and after about 5 minutes cross the footbridge on the right. Now keep a sharp lookout for the broken down stile* on the left where you join the main route.

The Main Route

Cross it and follow the well trodden track steeply up the wood to a stone step stile above. Now go up the long field keeping just to the right of the line of electricity poles to find the gate and the access road to Beatrix.

Beatrix is a strange name for a farm. It is not as you might think, a woman's name but a fairly modern corruption of the word Battrix which in turn is derived from the Irish-Norse name Batherarges. Close at hand Gamble Hole is derived from Gamel, a Norse personal name, and was called Gammellsarges in the thirteenth century. Many areas of north-west England were settled by Irish-Norse people from both Dublin and the Isle of Man in the ninth and tenth centuries who left their mark in the place's name, for example, Grimsargh, Goosnargh, and Anglezarke, spelt Andlesargh in the eighteenth century.

Follow the access road round the back of the farm buildings and when it starts to curve into the house yard go through the right-hand one of two gates. (This is not the right of way as shown on the map but its use has the farmer's approval. You join the right of way route in about 25 yards.) Climb up steeply then bear left towards the fence following it all the way into Oxenhurst Clough. The descent into the clough is steep and rough: keep at least in sight of the fence for the rickety little gate you need is close to it. Keep straight ahead on a faint path that eventually joins the fence line and leave the wooded clough by another rickety gate. Continue straight ahead and following the fence cum line of hawthorn bushes to emerge onto a tarmac access road within sight of The Hey.

This house has an interesting stone mounted outside for all to see. Four names are incised into it, Richard and Ann Alison with the date 1784 and the names of the present owners and the date 1984. Almost certainly the first couple built the house, for the late eighteenth century was a time of enclosure of marginal land to feed the growing population of England. The stone was originally set into the end wall of the house and hidden by a stable. Recent house extenstions revealed it and it was moved and set in its present position.

Continue along the roughly tarmacked access road to Burn House, about $1/2$ mile, and when you have gone round the sharp bend just beyond the house bear left across the field making for a point just below the barn to find a stone step stile. (New fences have been erected in this large field and the right of way route does not align with that shown on the OS map, but there are no problems.) The ground beyond the stile was ploughed in 1989 so follow the path round the ploughed part to the fence on the right then continue left to the stile. Now aim for the gate ahead where you will find yourself on a wide gravel road. Turn right and follow it to the end of the fence. Turn left here and follow the fence right over the hill keeping straight on to the road at Laythams.

Turn left on the road and in about 5 minutes turn left into the newly tarmacked track that leads to Burn Side Cottage. Keep right at the cottage through a gate marked with a blue arrow and continue through the goat's pen to another waymarked gate then into a vast field that runs up to the base of the fell. Keep near the wall to start with and when you see a stake on the left cross the wet hollow to find a narrow path on a raised ridge of good grass. It will lead you right up this rough wet field to the fell gate at the top.

A deep cut hollow track now leads to the right, makes a sharp turn left and continues up the fell right to Dunsop Head. At the corner pause to enjoy the wide view over Stocks Reservoir, then where the track splits, take the left-hand one. As the track curves round to the head of the valley there are again fine views towards Stocks Reservoir but as you approach the wall at Dunsop Head the track disappears in a wet green morass. Deal with this as best you can and keep on to the gate, which is further than you think.

From the gate a well trodden peaty track marked with an unnecessary number of yellow topped poles lead you down to the end of the shooting track above Whitendale Farm. Then follow this cart-track down to the gate into the farmyard.**

As you start the descent there is a fine view of the fells to the west. Just across the valley is the low but shapely Middle Knoll and behind it the higher Whins Fell over which an old track goes to the Trough road.

Whitendale to Dunsop Bridge

Immediately before a gate turn left into the field. A pleasant green track soon appears and leads you all the way down the valley by the riverside. At first it is poised high above the river then as it starts to drop it forks. Take the upper one - unless you like a bit of excitement. Both tracks come down to a former Fylde Water Board hut. Now you walk along the riverside with its deep dark pools fringed with oak, rowan, and birch, a fine sight glowing with colour on a good autumn afternoon. Make the most of it, for this enjoyable green track joins the tarmac road at a bridge. This road is a waterworks road used as a picnic footpath and has little if any traffic. It is not without its pleasures - you will surely see plenty of rabbits diving for cover into the bracken, you will scare many a pheasant - yourself too, if their raucous metallic cry catches you unawares. Keep an eye on the river as it winds about but simply follow the road straight to Dunsop Bridge. Turn left over the bridge to return to your car.

**Extension to Brennand Farm

If you are doing the extension go through the gate and straight ahead to the road. Turn right to find the bridge some few yards upstream. Cross it and go very steeply up the field. There's scarcely any path to be seen but shortly you will reach a deep grassy groove.

Follow it and from its end a path emerges leading you to a small gate in a wall. Passing through this, turn left for about 100 yards then bear right to one of the many yellow topped stakes on this route. The gradient now eases but to offset this the path passes through a big area of rushes, very wet indeed. Many pathlets go through it trying to avoid the worst... Take your pick and make for the corner of the fence ahead.

You may be surprised to see that this fence encloses a sizeable rectangular pond, now almost totally overgrown with reeds. It once supplied water to the lead mine whose spoil heaps you pass a little further on. Lead was mined here as early as the mid seventeenth century but the water supply and large spoil heaps probably date from 1865 when the Whitendale Mining Co. mined lead at Sykes, Brennand and Whitendale. Mining ceased in 1873 when the price of lead dropped below the economic level.

Carry on to the stile and then down the field to the corner where big spoil heaps can be seen the other side of the wall.

Before you quite reach the stile in the corner there are two small grass grown spoil heaps on the left. In one of them an industrious rabbit has scratched out a large amount of clinker and coke, the residues of some boiler house now demolished.

Pass between the big spoil heaps to find the cart-track and gate. The cart-track continues and a little way along a branch goes off to the right. Follow this right down to Brennand Farm.

Brennand is yet another name derived from Irish-Norse meaning the burning one. By a long tradition there was a chapel here in the Middle Ages. At one time a stone with five crosses carved on it stood by the door, but it is now built into the altar of Whalley Abbey Conference House.

Keep straight ahead through the farm-yard and follow the farm road passing Lower Brennand Farm. Keep right at the junction beyond it to join the route from Whitendale at the bridge close to the waterworks building.

Extension to the Trough Road from Brennand Farm

Turn right past the farmhouse and enter the field by a small gate. Continue to the large field where there is no path to speak of. Just aim for the gate as soon as it can be seen. From it a well defined path, Ouster Rake, takes you easily up the fell side. It is built up in places with properly constructed bridges over the small streams, evidence of its being used as a packhorse track, confirmed by the word Rake. The path again disappears in the large field but a line of yellow topped stakes guides you in the right direction towards the clump of trees surrounding the ruins of Trough House. From here a well defined stony track takes you down to the road where you turn left to reach the car parking area at Langden Brook.

A Note about Dunsop Bridge

Dunsop Bridge was once part of the hamlet of Beatrix, now a solitary farm higher up the fell, which from the thirteenth to the eighteenth century was a place of some local importance, holding regular markets. Then, as roads became more important in the life of a community, Beatrix diminished in importance. Dunsop Bridge was at the junction of the road leading to Slaidburn and other important villages and the Trough of Bowland road. This was an ancient route of considerable importance, used by judges journeying between the Law Courts at Lancaster and York; indeed, in 1616 the Pendle Witches travelled to Lancaster for their trial by this route.

The hamlet increased in size in the early to mid nineteenth century as a result of the lead mining activity on the fells between Whitendale and Brennand, and other places in the area, having a blacksmith's shop which is now the local garage. Just outside the village on the Trough road is the Roman Catholic church aptly dedicated to St Hubert, patron saint of foresters. It was built by the Townley family who had made a fortune from racehorses, one of theirs Kettledrum having won the Derby in 1861. The white marble angel in front of the church, now grey-green with moss and algae, is a memorial to Richard Henry Townley. Dunsop Bridge's claim to fame today is that it is the nearest village to the centre of the British Isles and in 1992 British Telecom installed their 100,000th payphone there to celebrate.

WALKING THE HODDER TO SLAIDBURN   Walk 2.8

The title is, perhaps, a rather devious one as the river is not walked as a continuous length but in sections on both the outward and return routes. Taking in pastures and a little bit of fell, with good and varied views, it is one of the best shortish walks in the area with few route finding problems.

Category: B
Time: 4¹/₂-5 hours
Distance: 10
Maps: Pathfinder Series No.669 Chipping and Clitheroe and No.660
             Slaidburn and Forest of Bowland (SD64/74 and SD65/75)
Start at: Dunsop Bridge car park

Dunsop Bridge to Giddy Bridge

Leave the car park by the left-hand exit and turn into the drive to
Thorneyholme Hall, now a health farm. Cross the bridge and turn
right along the river bank *before* entering the hotel grounds. At the
first gate leave the cart-track you are on and follow the river bank
downstream through several fields until the river starts to pull
away to the right. At this point the chimneys of Burholme are just
visible. Then keep straight ahead through two fields before bearing
left towards Burholme. Immediately before the gate leading to the
footbridge turn left up Fielding Clough and continue to the second
stile. After crossing it turn left and follow a faint path by the fence
to its end. Then continue by this faint path all the way up the
roughish fellside more or less following the stream. Do not be led
astray by a wide track crossing the stream on an embankment. You
will come to a ladder stile onto the open fell - giant tussock country
criss-crossed by many tiny tracks. The path continues for a little
while but soon disintegrates. The problem is then to find the right
fragment, for there is no clear path to the gate on the other side of the
moor. When you have gained enough height to see the trees ahead
bear right, and when more trees appear well to the right aim
midway between the two clumps to find the gate.

*There's a fine view ahead to the high ground behind Settle. On a good
day you may even pick out the distinctive hump of Pen-y-Ghent and the
Hodder valley is at your feet with the river winding its way in seductive
curves. Knowlmere Manor is not yet in sight, but this splendid looking
many gabled house is a Victorian rebuilding of the ancient manor house
which goes back to the thirteenth century.*

You will see a barn below on your right. Go steeply down the
field keeping well to its left to locate the remains of a stile just below
a solitary hawthorn tree. Continue straight down the field to the
next stile, then a gate leads you to the access road to Knowlmere

Manor where you turn right to reach Giddy Bridge, a pleasant place for lunch if the time of day be right.

Giddy Bridge to Slaidburn

Continue along this rough road to the tarmac road, turn left and, shortly after crossing Foulscales brook, turn left into the fields just beyond a deserted farm. Bear right and uphill a little to find a gate in the hedge, then drop down through two fields to reach the banks of the Hodder again. Follow the path to the road at Newton Bridge.

A short diversion takes you into Newton itself, an ancient village containing many seventeenth- and eighteenth-century houses with datestones to prove it. The pub, handily the nearest building to the river, is a striking Georgian building, and opposite it is an even finer well proportioned Georgian house. On the main street is the Old School House, endowed by a John Brabbin in 1768 for the instruction of Quaker children. Newton was the home village of the Quaker movement in the Bowlands and its most famous son was John Bright, the nineteenth-century reformer.

Cross Newton Bridge and turn into the field on the other side. A well trodden and signed path leads onto the very bank of the river, here usually dark and still, then cuts off a bend to enter a wood at the foot of a little limestone cliff, the edge of one of the reef knolls found around the Hodder. Just beyond, it fades out but you continue to join a cart-track which will lead you to the road about 1/2 mile from Slaidburn and in sight of the church.

Slaidburn to Dunsop Bridge

In the village (see About Slaidburn), turn left in front of the Hark to Bounty (open all day all the year round) and continue through the village climbing steadily up the hill until you come to some farm buildings on the left in about 1/2 mile. Turn left along the access road to Pain Hill Farm (it is signed), enjoying wide views of the steep sided bracken covered fells to your right as you go. Pain Hill, a plain double fronted building with a datestone 1689 over the door, is the farm where John Brennand the founder of Slaidburn's school lived. Turn right in front of the house then left at the end of the barn onto a gravel track into the fields. At its end follow the wall to reach Crawshaw where a little care is needed to find the way to the road. Turn left into the yard, pass behind the barn, and enter the field by a gate directly opposite its vast door. The first stile is to the right and there are two more in line. After crossing the second one of these head diagonally left across the crown of the field to find the stile in the corner. Then turn right and head for the road, jumping the little brook at the stone slab.

Opposite, tucked away in a corner, is the stile you need. Follow the wall then the hedge cum fence directly down, passing through a rough boggy area, to the access road to Heaning. Go straight across it, pass by the side of their trout farm to a gate, and continue straight ahead to reach the Dunsop Bridge-Slaidburn road at a stile. Turn right on the road and follow it for a short ½ mile passing all the buildings and then turn left at a "Public Footpath" sign into a cobbled yard. Leave it by a little gate and follow the cart-track down through the fields towards a footbridge. Cross this highly entertaining bridge and turn downstream to follow the best bit of riverside walking on this stretch of the Hodder. You will come in sight of a concrete waterworks bridge painted a ghastly pastel green. There is no right of way across it but the gates are not locked, so cross to the other side to continue downstream as close to the river as a stretch of boggy ground permits. A strip of woodland forces you away from the river. Look out for the stile into it and, having crossed a side stream, leave it by a not very obvious stile to your right. Now cut across the large field aiming to the right of the bridge to find the exit gate onto Thorneyholme's drive where you turn right and reach your car in 2 minutes.

ABOVE THE HODDER VALLEY   Walk 2.9

This walk starts along a sort of terrace high above the Hodder which runs along the foot of the fells from Hareden to Dinkling Green Farm, and has fine views of the river in places. (This length of path is also used by Walk 1.4.) The route then cuts across, again above the Hodder, to Burholme Bridge and returns on the banks of the Hodder to Dunsop Bridge.

Category: B
Time: about 4 hours
Distance: 8½ miles

Maps: Pathfinder Series No.669 Chipping and Clitheroe and No.660
           Slaidburn and Forest of Bowland (SD64/74 and SD65/75)
Start at: Dunsop Bridge car park

The Car Park to Hareden Farm

Turn right on leaving the car park and right again as you come to the
first river bridge. Follow this quiet road to its end at the houses and
continue through a snicket gate behind them, following the path to
the footbridge which you then cross. Turn left on the road and right
into the field just before you reach Closes Barn Farm. There's no
path, just a few animal tracks which you follow through the gate
into the second field. Then make well to the right to find the signed
exit gate by a telegraph pole. Turn right on the road and after about
10 minutes turn left into the private road to Hareden Farm, a
secluded hamlet of picturesque houses in a beautiful valley.

Hareden Farm to Dinkling Green Farm

Continue along the road to the group of houses, turn right over the
bridge and when you've crossed the stream yet again go over the
ladder stile on the left. The path is faint: climb up and to the left to
find another ladder stile besides a gate. Here you find yourself on
a gravel cart-track, but it is not for you. At once bear to the right and
go up to the top of this long field (which runs almost to the top of
Mellor Knoll), where you will find a gate and stile in the corner. A
track continues but soon splits up and disappears. A yellow topped
pole to the right gives you a clue as to the line to follow and another
rather distant one puts you in line for the even more distant ladder
stile.

Never mind the bull that may be in the next field, he'll be more
interested in his heifers than you, at least he was when I went
through. Just look around you and enjoy the widening view over
the Hodder Valley. Now a wide but barely visible track drops
gently down towards the band of broadleaved woodland that
encircles the head of a great hollow of the fells. It gives superb views
of the Hodder with the river making silvery curves in the lush
meadows below whilst beyond, the mast of Waddington Fell breaks
the horizon. The path becomes better marked and follows the
boundary wall of the wood to a little gate and continues inside the

Tower Lodge, Trough of Bowland
The Great Stone of Fourstones

Clougha seen from the Lancaster road

The bridge at Holmes Barn, Hindburndale

woodland for a while. When it breaks out of the wood the fire break of the conifer plantation is straight ahead. The path continues through it, dull, wet, and without views of any sort for a short $^{1}/_{2}$ mile. When it emerges keep straight ahead for a few minutes to meet a tarmac lane by some hen cabins. Turn left and then right at the junction ahead to reach Higher Fence Farm just below. (If you want to shorten the walk for any reason, simply follow the left branch at the junction. Turn left onto a faint path at the corner after passing a disused quarry, cross the stile in the corner of the field and follow the fence on the right to the road. Turn left there, and you will reach Burnholme Bridge in about 25 minutes.)

Go straight through the farmyard, cross the stream then leave the cart-track turning left down the narrow field and leave it by a stile on the right. Dinkling Green Farm is now in sight: pass to the right of the house then bear left passing between two barns. At their end turn sharp left and pass between more farm buildings, cross the bridge and follow the farm's access road to the public road. It winds along the foot of a collection of rocky knolls and has fine views across to Burnslack, Fair Oak Fell, and Wolf Fell.

These rocky knolls are the most westerly ones of a series of reef knolls that extend westwards from near Grassington, a contrast with the gritstone of the Bowland Fells themselves.

Dinkling Green Farm to Burholme Bridge

Keep straight ahead on the public road for about 400 yards when you will see a stile on the left into a narrow field. In the next field head to the right of the hamlet of Fair Oak to enter the stockyard. On the left, note the barn has a datestone of 1726, typical of many of the Bowland farms. Continue straight ahead passing between the two houses into the field where a muddy track continues for some distance. At its end cut across to the right following the fence round a considerable curve to find the next stile, then keep straight ahead to a stile at the foot of a limestone reef knoll. Bear diagonally right over the lower shoulder of the knoll, keeping your height above the wood, to pick up a cart-track which will bring you to New Laund Farm, a name redolent of the times when the Leagram deer park extended in this direction. Now follow their access road to the public road, turn right and a few minutes sees you at the elegant span of Burholme Bridge.

Burholme Bridge to Dunsop Bridge on the Banks of the Hodder

Cross the bridge and take the farm access road on the left to Burholme Farm where you turn left immediately after the house. Cross a little footbridge, and once you are in the field bear right following a broad green cart-track when you have reached the lower part of the field. At a little metal gate it shrinks to a footpath and reaches the bank of the Hodder. Now continue upstream close to the river bank, all the way to Thorneyholme Hall, a large Victorian style of establishment on the river bank, and now a health farm. Sometimes the path is well trodden, at other times it is very faint, and always there is fine riverside scenery. Keep to the left of the farm buildings as you approach the hall and cross the bridge to reach the road not 50 yards from the car park.

STARTING AT WHITEWELL

A WALK THROUGH THE RADHOLME DEER PARK

Walk 2.10

The higher ground above the Whitewell on the east side of the Hodder has some very attractive walking, mainly through upland pastures with a variety of good views and a particularly fine finish. Its historical background is a bonus. Route finding is not easy between the first and second crossings of the Whitewell-Doeford Bridge road.

Category:	B
Length:	8 miles
Time:	4-5½ hours depending on what route finding problems you may have
Map:	Pathfinder Series No.669 Chipping and Clitheroe (SD64/74)
Start at:	The Inn at Whitewell. Parking is permitted in the field behind the church, reached by the obvious cart-track.

Cross the road, pass the black and white painted building and go up the obvious steps a little further along the road. Carry on up the field towards the house, and when you reach their access road turn right, if briefly, along it. At the apparent mini-railway tunnel - actually part of the former Fylde Water Board's works, bear right and continue along the well used cart-track to the end of the field. Here go through the upper of two gates, turn right along the wall and then the fence (which is not marked on the OS map,) and follow it through two large fields. Longridge Fell - and how well it is named - soon fills the view straight ahead and in springtime lapwings, curlews, and oystercatchers abound in these fields. If you look below you as you pass through the first two of these fields you will see a bank and ditch, thought to be the boundary of the Radholme deer park in the twelfth and thirteenth centuries.

In Norman times most of England was still quite heavily forested and deer, wolves, and wild boar roamed freely, hunted by the nobility for food and pleasure. After the passage of a couple of centuries many trees had been felled, and much land was used for the rearing of cattle. This lead to a decline in the value of the land as a hunting ground and in order to conserve the deer, launds or deer parks were established. These were large areas surrounded by a deep ditch and bank on which stood a fence of stakes or pales, and in which the deer could be kept free from marauders. Some of them could then be released into the forest for the purposes of hunting as and when required. Radholme Laund was one of two in this area, the other being Chipping Laund. Its useful life was over by the sixteenth century, the land then being rented as pasture for cattle.

At the second swing gate take a long diagonal line across the field aiming at a strip of woodland by the roadside to the right, and reach the road by a gate with a footpath signpost.

Turn left on the road and back into the fields at the right-hand end of the wood. Set off aiming just to the right of the right-hand one of three electricity poles, pass above the isolated trees and then aim at the corner of the wood. Now follow the wood to the stile and gate below. A delightful view of the River Hodder awaits you. Continue by a sort of hollow way that snakes across the field. It is almost certainly the boundary of the deer park again, you're walking on historic ground hereabouts. After you've forded a little stream ahead which can be difficult after heavy rain, go through the gate to the left, then through the next one in the corner of the field ahead.

Now walk parallel to the lower fence to reach a gate by a stout oak tree, continue in the same direction until you have crossed a tiny stream, then climb steadily up the hillside aiming at a solitary tree. You will reach a gate, but don't go through it. Instead turn left and follow the fence dropping down a little to find the stile in the fence which runs down the hillside. Having crossed the stile follow the fence into the short lane leading to Lower Lees. The house is worth a closer look if you are interested in old houses.

There are several houses in the immediate area with variations on the name Lees, and it is believed that they were in existence at the time of the Domesday book, 1086. The house at Lower Lees was re-built in the seventeenth-century, having a datestone of 1678 over the door. The ground floor mullioned windows and the doorway have a continuous string moulding above them, an unusual functional cum decorative feature, for the string moulding kept the rain off the windows.

Turn right in the lane and left at the junction to reach the next farm where you go into the field on the right to pass it. Continue through the wood, then gently drop down to the footbridge but do not cross it. Carry on upstream a few yards to a small gate leading to a fenced path which takes you onto the road.

Now turn right and in a few yards turn left at the junction. In about ¼ mile you will come to a sharp bend and 20 yards beyond it turn right into the access road to Lee House Farm.

This 20 yard length is part of the Roman road that ran across Bowland from Ribchester to Burrow in Lonsdale. The lane that joins the road at the sharp bend is the continuation to the south-west and to the north-east it is buried under the tarmac. A glance at the OS map shows the line it followed across the fells.

Pause to look at the house on the right, another of the ancient houses of this part of Bowland.

Lee House is another seventeenth-century house, rather tucked away in a corner of farm buildings. Again it has mullioned windows, and again a datestone of 1678. The door lintel is unusual, with three small arches carved in it.

Then having passed a large cylindrical blue tank, go left into a small field cluttered with agricultural implements to find the stile into the wood behind the house. The track continues into the wood becoming very steep indeed and slippery. Just lurch from tree to tree down the garlic and bluebell filled wood, quite spectacular. A good new bridge awaits you at the bottom, and after crossing the stile beyond, a notice faces you. Not the Keep Out sort, far from it, but an announcement that this is an Open Access Area, agreed between the Countryside Commission and Browsholme Hall Estates. Turn right to follow the stream until you have crossed a stile over a substantial fence. Now turn left and work your way up the steep hillside to the stile at the top. Get your breathe whilst you recognise Waddington/Easington Fell straight ahead then continue to the barn where you pick up the track leading to Micklehurst. The right of way path goes through the gate leading to the front of the house, but it is better to continue along this track to reach their access road between the buildings.

Turn left and follow the road to the point where it starts to swing right. Here go through the gate on the left, pass the electricity pole and bear left steeply down to the road at Mill Brook Bridge. Turn left and continue along the road to the entrance road to Browsholme Hall, guarded by a fine lodge. Turn into this road and almost at once turn left on a cart-track that runs up this long field parallel to the wood. Where it turns right keep straight ahead through the gate and continue to the gate and stile just to the right of the wood. At the gate at the end of the wood bear diagonally right to reach a rough little field and keep a lookout for Browsholme Spire ahead. It looks for all the world like a church, but as you will see, it isn't.

In this small very rough field pass the little pond on its left and leave it on the left by a stile between a pair of stone gateposts. At the end of the bit of woodland bear right towards the spire. By degrees it becomes clear that it is merely a length of wall, though crenelated, stuck on the end of a house. Those curious looking arches turn out to be no more than the framework of a ruined green house. You'll find the stile fairly close to the wood and you now follow its edge to find the stile into the field. A surprise view awaits you as you reach the highest point on this walk: Totridge and all the other fells behind come into view. Cross the farm access road and then bear slightly right dropping down a little as you approach the road. You'll come to a piece of new forestry that was out of sight, and a stile gives you access to a little path through it that takes you to the road.

Browsholme Spire

Straight across is the access road to Crimpton with a reassuring footpath sign. Go along this to the house, note the row of narrow windows in its upper storey, a sign that handloom weaving was once carried on here. Go straight through the farmyard into the field and follow the fence to its end, then bear left up the field to find the stile and track through the forestry in the re-entrant corner. It is very wet in places, but eventually you emerge to a good view with Whitewell not far below. Over the wall you will see a clump of trees in the middle of the field below. In their centre is Hell Hole Pot, an open shaft some 45ft deep. Head to the right of the trees but divert a little to see the shaft at the bottom of a deep hollow. It is easily and safely inspected provided you don't cross the fence. Continue down the field bearing left to reach a good stile near the gate, then further down the field you will find a gate cum stile onto the road.

Go through the gate opposite, noting the old lime kiln and the quarry above that supplied it with limestone for now you are walking on the Chatburn Limestone. Continue around the curve of the hillside to a gate in a corner on the far side. Go through this to the house you passed when you started, and from it retrace your steps to the road.

A Note about Browsholme

Browsholme (pronounced Brusom) Hall is the only ancient house in Bowland open to the public and is well worth a visit, though it is most unlikely it could be incorporated with this walk as it is only open on Saturdays in June, July and August and occasional other dates between April and September. The house was built early in the sixteenth century by one Edward Parker and has been the Parker family's home ever since. The head of the family holds the hereditary title of Bowbearer of the Forest of Bowland, who was second in command to the Keeper of the Forest. The building is not an elaborate one, being in the shape of the letter H, in the style of the times. The entrance hall is hung with ancient weapons and armour, heads of deer, and is sparsely furnished with heavily carved oak chests and cupboards. It is very atmospheric and particularly fine, whilst the rest of the house is of a more domesticated nature, suited to the family whose home the house still is. A member of the family takes parties of visitors round the house.

Browsholme Spire was built before the days of landrover access to the fells to guide people who were out shooting back to the hall. Originally it had a gothic arch in it, possibly the source of the name.

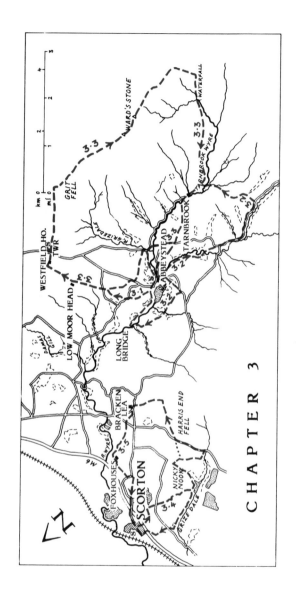

Chapter 3

WALKS AROUND WYRESDALE AND ITS FELLS

3.1   Around Abbeystead, Category C
3.2   Following the River Wyre, Category B
3.3   Grit Fell and Ward's Stone to Tarnbrook, Category A
3.4   Nicky Nook direct from Scorton, Category C+
3.5   Grise Dale and Harrisend Fell, Category B

AROUND ABBEYSTEAD   Walk 3.1

Abbeystead, like Bleasdale, is a scattered parish with a school and church whose heart is the picturesque estate buildings close to the lake. These were built by the 7th Earl of Sefton when he built Abbeystead Hall, hidden in the trees above Marshaw Wyre, but well seen on Walk 3.2. There is a public telephone but little else in the hamlet. It takes its name from the Cistercian abbey that is supposed to have been founded there but failed to become established. This walk has a look at the little hamlet by pleasant field paths with good views of Tarnbrook Fell on the return. Most of the stiles are waymarked.

Category: C
Time: about 2 hours if time is spent at Meeting House Farm
Distance: 3½ miles
Map: Pathfinder Series No.659 Galgate and Dolphinholme (SD45/55)
Start at: Stoops Bridge, Abbeystead

Approaching from Dolphinholme go through the hamlet and as soon as you have passed the school you cross Stoops Bridge. Immediately turn right through a pair of stone gateposts, the entrance to Doeholme, and there is room for a few cars on the right. From the Trough road turn left into Long Lane and the road is on the left about 70 yards beyond the entrance to Abbeystead Hall. Often full on Sundays.

Abbeystead to Meeting House Farm

Return to the bridge, turn left and go through the tiny hamlet of Abbeystead. There's a school and a phone box and not much else besides a few estate houses, for the land around here belongs to the Duke of Westminster. Walk up the road on the left-hand side - against all safety recommendations I know - but this side gives excellent views of Abbeystead Lake, strictly speaking reservoir, but it's a very natural looking sheet of water, fringed with reeds and beloved of wild duck. You'll almost certainly hear them quacking or see them dashing about the water.

The Lake was built in the 1840s, when Lancaster Corporation impounded the headwaters of the River Wyre to slake the thirst of its growing population. It supplied compensation water to the many mills downstream, and for this reason is natural looking, as its level does not change as does that of reservoirs. Unfortunately there is no public access to its banks.

At the corner of the road at the top of the hill go through the stile on the left. Go straight ahead to the left of the left-hand shed then go slightly right to the field corner ahead, follow the line of hawthorn trees straight ahead, bear right to cross the stream on a good footbridge and climb up the field to the left of the church. Go into the churchyard by a little gate, spare a moment to have a look at the church then leave it by a stile in the opposite corner immediately turning right to reach the road.

Here turn left and in about 100 yards go right through a gate with a public footpath sign but no waymark. Go up the field on the right-hand side of the hedge, turn left when you come to the fence at the top of the field. Follow this fence crossing a stile on the way until you come to a poor stile in the fence on your right. Clamber over it and cross the field to the top of the wood where a step stile over a new wooden fence takes you to the large stone in the wall that passes for a stile. Then cut across to the right of the farm buildings to find a little bridge onto a nettle infested path. Turn left over the stile and you are at Meeting House Farm.

The Meeting House was behind the large house on the right as you cross the stile and is now part of it. It was originally a simple single storey building with a stable at the end, now used as a garage. Towards the end of the nineteenth century the Quaker community in Far Wyresdale built a school adjoining the Meeting House and this is now the house. The schoolmaster's house was the white house across the yard from the school but in those days it was much smaller. The burial ground lies behind the former Meeting House and can still be used by members of the local Quaker community. There is public access to it through a small gate in the yard of the house. It is very different from the usual churchyard. Its small simple headstones, all to the same design, bear the names of only half a dozen families, buried in family groups.

Meeting House Farm to Grisedale Bridge

Now re-cross the stile by which you arrived and carry on down the wallside - the wall of the graveyard - to a footbridge. Continue in the same direction, ignoring the waymarks, they are misleading, until you can see the gate then make towards it. Now head for the corner of the field and, as soon as you can see it, bear left for the gate and Chapel House Farm. The name strongly suggests that there was a chapel there at some time, but the house, probably early eighteenth century, shows no sign of it today.

At the entrance to the farmyard turn left through a waymarked gate, head below the house to find the stile and continue to the road. Turn right and after about 200 yards turn left through a gate onto a wide farm track that crosses a tiny stream in a dip and then disappears. Carry on straight ahead to the corner of the fence, follow it for a 100 yards or so then cross over to the other side. From here onwards you get fine views of the Tarnbrook Fells. Follow the fence through a huge field, once two fields, judging by the remains of an iron ladder stile. At the next stile make toward the barn for quite a time then gradually drop down to the right towards a line of trees. Go below them and continue to find the stile in the wall just beyond a gate at Grisedale Bridge.

Grisedale Bridge to Abbeystead

Go through the gate and follow the cart-track right through this very pleasant bit of park-like land: the further you go the better it gets as it meets then follows the river, the Tarnbrook Wyre, and gives views of a fine house with commanding views of the river. It brings you onto the road at Abbeystead at Stoops Bridge. A quick left and right brings you to your car.

FOLLOWING THE RIVER WYRE   Walk 3.2

Two major streams, the Tarnbrook Wyre and the Marshaw Wyre
unite in Abbeystead Lake from which emerges the River Wyre
proper. Ideally this walk would start at Long Bridge, but there is no
convenient parking place so it starts at Stoops Bridge, Abbeystead,
and first goes downstream to Long Bridge by field paths high above
the river. It then follows the Wyre upstream passing Abbeystead
Lake to reach Stoops Bridge from where it continues up the Marshaw
Wyre as far as Tower Lodge, some 3 miles. The walk then goes over
the fell to Tarnbrook and returns to Abbeystead through the fields
paying but lip service to the Tarnbrook Wyre. Obviously the walk
may be split into two parts if convenient.

Category:	B for the entire walk or the second part, C for the first part
Time:	5-5½ hours for the entire walk, a short 2 hours for Abbeystead to Long Bridge, 3½ for the other half
Distance:	a total of 10 miles, 3½ for the shorter walk
Maps:	Pathfinder Series No.659 Galgate and Dolphinholme and No.660 Slaidburn and Forest of Bowland (SD56/56, SD65/75) which is used only for about ½ mile above Tower Lodge and is hardly necessary if attention is paid to the text.
Start at:	Stoops Bridge, Abbeystead. See the previous walk for instructions for finding it.

From Stoops Bridge to Long Bridge by Cam Clough and Catshaw Hall

Facing the river turn left on leaving your car and continue along the
road until you have crossed the Marshaw Wyre. Immediately turn
right into the woods on a well used path signed with a yellow
waymarker. These useful waymarks continue all the way to the
road at Haythornthwaite Farm, and instructions are barely necessary.

*Pause to marvel at the jungle of Japanese knotweed that fills the wet
places in the base of the woods. It must have been all of 10ft high in the
summer of 1992.*

You will find the next waymark in a few minutes pointing up a
steep set of old stone steps. At their top turn right, leave the wood
by a stile and continue towards the farm shortly in view. Bear left to
the gate poised just above the stream and follow the path to the road.

Turn right towards the farm buildings and take the farm road that crosses the cattle grid, continuing on it to Marl House.

Go past the house and buildings into the field to the next gate then continue straight ahead eventually keeping just to the right of a line of trees to find the stile and footbridge over Cam Brook, a large fast flowing stream. A set of stone steps leads from the bridge up to a green, level, ridge. Turn right on it and follow it to its end close to some ruins utterly overgrown by trees. Turn left and follow a faint path up to a little gate out of the wood.

The level green ridge is the embankment of a former millpond that impounded the waters of Cam Brook for Catshaw Mill, a water powered worsted spinning mill probably built towards the end of the eighteenth century. If you look upstream from where you join it you will see that it extended a considerable distance, capturing a side stream. The basin of the pond is obvious enough.

Continue across the field to find another white painted bridge in the small tree filled ravine ahead (not shown on the OS map) then continue straight ahead along the fence to pick up the access road to Little Catshaw and Catshaw Hall.

Both of them are fine buildings, the former with a datestone of 1763 and the square windows that were the style of those times, the Hall with a datestone of 1668, still with mullioned and transomed windows but fairly heavily restored.

Here go straight through the farmyard into the field taking in the good views up the valley to the fells. Go straight down the field to the corner of the wood to find a well graded if muddy track that leads comfortably down to a stile and footbridge. Go through the wood, turn right and drop down to Long Bridge.

Long Bridge to Abbeystead

Long Bridge is at the mouth of a little gorge that simply invites exploration but there is no right of way. Upstream there is, and you just walk through this very long riverside field until you have to join a hard core road that becomes concreted.

This length of riverside is very fine indeed. The river is young enough to brawl merrily along, the right-hand bank is steep and well wooded, a picture in autumn, but the left-hand one where you walk is open pasture land.

Continue along the concrete road for about 150 yards passing a modern stone building on your left.

This is the water pumping station, rebuilt after that horrifying explosion on May 23rd 1984. A party of local people, mostly from St Michael's-on-Wyre were being shown round it one afternoon. Nine of them were killed outright and thirty injured, including the husband of a well known and respected local journalist, Pat Seed. Six of the injured died within a few days. The cause of the explosion was a mystery for some time, but was eventually traced to an accumulation of explosive methane gas carried by the peaty water.

When you come to a pair of poles carrying a mains transformer leave the road for the stile behind it and avoid the road. The path is poised above the river and has a good view of the wall of the curved dam towering high in the air, a fine sight in wet weather with brown peaty water curling over it in a steady curtain. Follow the path through the wood to a wide reddish painted gate where you join the concrete road. Follow it to a collection of farm buildings and turn right opposite the first one passing through a gate into the field. The stile onto the road is in the right-hand corner. Now walk down the road through the hamlet of Abbeystead to Stoops Bridge and your car. Keep a good look out to the right as you go down the road to get a view of the Lake, the only one you will get as there is no public access to its banks.

From Stoops Bridge to Tower Lodge

Turn into the road where you are parked and continue a few yards past the cars then left onto a wide rough cart-track. This bears a yellow waymark which appears at strategic points throughout this part of the walk. It continues into the field where you go right to its far end passing a shed to find the footbridge.

As you walk along the field you will have a fine view of Abbeystead Hall high on the hillside, sheltered by a belt of trees. It looks to be the sort of hall you would find in a fairy story - large, a bit higgledy piggledy with its gable ends, mullioned and transomed windows. Although it is Elizabethan in style it was built in 1886 by the Earl of Sefton who subsequently built many of the estate houses in Abbeystead. After the death of the 7th Earl in 1972 his widow continued to manage the estate until 1980 when it was sold to the present owner, the 6th Duke of Westminster. Today the house is only

Abbeystead Hall

used in summer by the Duke of Westminster and his family (the Grosvenor family) who from time to time open its fine grounds to the public in money raising events for charity. The rest of the time caretakers are in residence. From the long field beyond the footbridge you get glimpses of the gardens - if there are not too many leaves on the trees - trim paths in well kept lawns lead to tennis courts, herbaceous borders, and shrubberies.

Beyond the footbridge you enter a very long field, mostly trackless. Climb up the slope straight ahead and continue at this level. A comforting waymarker post confirms that you are on the right line and then the line of the path runs closer to the river mostly hidden in the wood but very audible if the weather is wet. There are gates and occasional footbridges across the river but most of them quite obviously are not for you. You will pass through the bottom end of a wood when you are approaching Hangington Clough and drop down to a single stone slab bridge. Now contour round the hillock ahead to find the bridge over the River Wyre. As you climb over the little bump ahead the character of the scenery changes almost instantly.

Up to this point you have walked through riverside pasture partly

Looking into the head of Wyresdale

enclosed by woodland, now you emerge into much more open ground with views of the dark mass of Haythornthwaite Fell across to the right. The change will be accentuated most of the way to Tower Lodge.

Rejoin the river, cross the clough by a little bridge, follow the side of the wood until it curves to the left then keep straight ahead to the gate and stile at the far corner of the field where you join the Trough road.

Keep straight on for a few minutes until you find a wooden ladder stile on the right marked with a white arrow, for this is a concessionary path, not a right of way. It is marked on the OS map as a faint dotted line, not easy to see, and runs between the road and the Marshaw Wyre past Marshaw Farm for almost a mile before rejoining the road. Then there is nothing for it but the road to Tower Lodge.

Traffic apart the road can be strikingly beautiful running close to the river almost the whole time. Its traffic hazard can be reduced by grass verges in many places. A long straggly stand of Scots pine looks quite dramatic on a lowering day, reminiscent of the Highlands. Just before you reach Tower Lodge a line of beech trees overhang the stream, breathtakingly beautiful on a golden October day. Tower Lodge, as its name suggests, was the lodge for the now ruinous Wyresdale Tower, which was built as a shooting box for a Henry Garnet, who owned the Abbeystead Estate.

At Tower Lodge, unmistakable in its faintly Gothic style, turn left onto the track that runs between the two buildings and follow it up the hill to a gate. About 100yds further on a waymark directs you away from the cart-track to the left. Avoid the attractive green cart-track and go much more steeply up the hillside, passing the concrete bases of what were probably wartime army huts, for the army made good use of the wild Bowlands during the war. Go through the broken down wall and the ladder stile comes into view to the left.

As you cross it the view to the Tarnbrook Fells opens up quite dramaticaly: at first Wards Stone, then Grit Fell to its left and the headwaters of the Tarnbrook Wyre to the right closed by the grassy shoulders of Wolf Hole Crag. This splendid panorama and its variations stays with you all the way down to Tarnbrook.

Keep going in the same direction, each stile is visible from the previous one and there are some waymarks for guidance. When you have crossed an iron stile, turn right down the wall side then follow the wall and the fence down the hill to a pair of fine stone built barns. Turn right through the gate and follow the track to Gilberton. Keep out of their stockyard, cross the footbridge over the Tarnbrook Wyre and join their access road which will take you to the tarmac road at Tarnbrook, once a considerably bigger hamlet than it is today.

From Tarnbrook to Abbeystead

Turn right on the tarmac road and walk through the hamlet for about 100 yards. Just beyond a gateway there is a large triangular area of grass on the right. Opposite there is a barn on a short walled lane. This is the start of the return through the fields and it can be identified beyond doubt by the big pine tree. Almost all stiles are waymarked with a discrete yellow arrow, a big help.

Beyond the gate there is a good bridge over the Tarnbrook Wyre, the last time you will see it until you are back at Stoops Bridge. (Note that this bridge is marked ford on Map No.659.) Cross it and turn right to cross a white painted ladder stile. The next ladder stile can be seen ahead almost at once. Once across the muddy lane follow the hedge to the barn seen ahead then bear diagonally right to find the correct stile. Cross the wide ditch then follow the fence to the corner. NOW KEEP STRAIGHT ON to find the stile in the trees. Do a quick left then right and follow the far side of the hedge to Top of Emmetts on the Trough road.

Go straight across the Trough road and cut behind Higher Emmetts to an electricity pole with a transformer box on it. Go straight ahead over the gate into a long field and make gradually left towards the wood and a stile in the far corner. This stile brings you into someone's garden. Respect their privacy and go straight ahead to the road. Continue down the hill to Abbeystead.

GRIT FELL & WARD'S STONE TO TARNBROOK   Walk 3.3

This walk takes advantage of the Access Area on Clougha and uses the Access Strip - a mere 12 metres wide - that links this Area to Tarnbrook passing over Grit Fell and Ward's Stone, at 516m the highest point in the Bowlands, and continuing over the fell to Tarnbrook. It gives the longest continuous stretch of moorland walking in either of the two Access Areas, about 8 miles, and given good visibility the views are without compare in the whole of the Bowlands. There is a path along the Access Strip and it is shown on the maps as a series of faint dotted lines. Note that you are supposed to keep to it. The return is by road or right of way field paths which give excellent walking but are apt to be time consuming.

Category:	A
Time:	6-7 hours
Distance:	13$\frac{1}{2}$ miles, about 1 mile less if the return by road is used
Maps:	Pathfinder Series No.659 Galgate and Dolphinholme and No.660 Slaidburn and Forest of Bowland (SD45/55 and SD65/75)
Start at:	the car park opposite Jubilee Tower which is marked on map No.659 and on the 1:50,000 Landranger map as Twr.

Approaches to the car park

1. From the south. Leave the M6 at junction 33, turn left on the A6 and almost immediately go left again. Having crossed the M6 turn right at the T-junction and in a good $\frac{1}{2}$ mile turn left at the crossroads. The road is signed Quernmore and Caton. Continue for about 4 miles and at the second crossroads turn right. It is easily identified by a telephone box. The Tower is about 2$\frac{1}{2}$

miles up the hill.

2. From the north leave the M6 at junction 34 turning right on the A683. Turn right on the Quernmore road on the outskirts of Caton and follow the signs to that place. Turn left up the hill immediately after Quernmore Post Office.

3. From East Lancashire travel via Clitheroe, Dunsop Bridge and the Trough of Bowland road. The Tower is on the left before the last steep descent.

From the car park to Ward's Stone

Before you start, assuming you have good visibility, it is worth going up the Tower, built as so many were to celebrate Queen Victoria's Diamond Jubilee. It has the edge over the car park's view over the coast.

Far away to the left-hand end of Morecambe Bay are Pilling and Fleetwood. You may even see Blackpool Tower on their left. Then there is a stretch of coast without any distinguishing features until you come to the Lune Estuary with Glasson Dock on the left-hand bank. If the tide is in a sinuous finger of water stretches right into the heart of Lancaster, a reminder that in the eighteenth century Lancaster was a major port trading with America and the West Indies. Next comes Heysham with its nuclear power station and then the town of Morecambe. Between Morecambe and Clougha stands Lancaster, easily picked out by the green dome of the Ashton Memorial. Across the wide curve of the bay lies Grange-over-Sands with the Lake District hills behind it. To the left of them is the hump of Black Combe and further left still, on an incredibly long finger of land, is Barrow in Furness. Whether the tide is in or not the sands are always wet and the Bay a subtle pattern of shades of blue merging to grey or to brown splashed with brilliant streaks of light. It is magnificent.

In the car park there is a discrete plaque near the Access Area map. It describes the finding of the Quernmore Burial in 1973 when this car park was being excavated. Briefly, the scant remains of a man were found buried in a split hollowed out oak tree. He was wrapped in a woollen shroud which was remarkably well preserved and is one of the very few pieces of cloth surviving from the Dark Ages. Radiocarbon dating assigned it to the seventh century. The conserved remains are displayed in Lancaster City Museum.

A path leaves the car park following the boundary fence to the top of Grit Fell passing a large cairn known as Shooters Pile near the top.

Grit Fell gives you your first views of the Yorkshire Dales peaks. Ingleborough is bold and quite unmistakable whilst Whernside to its left, despite its greater height, seems relatively insignificant. Looking further left you will see Gragareth and Great Coum then the steep sided Barbon Fell.

From just beyond the stile a well trodden peaty track waymarked with poles at wide intervals drops gently down to the dip between Grit Fell and Ward's Stone. Here it crosses a "vehicular access track" as the notice that warns you to keep off it calls it. Your track continues, boggy in places, to the first trig point on Ward's Stone, for this flat topped moor is blessed with two trig points, proof, if any were needed, of the wide views it offers. Here a number of boulders will give shelter from the wind for lunch whilst you enjoy fine views of Ingleborough. Continue to the second trig point - and the true top by just one metre - by dry easy walking on thready tracks marked by a few cairns.

Ward's Stone to Tarnbrook

Here the track turns right for a short time and passes a large boulder that should give really good shelter on a bad day provided the wind is in the west. The views over the Bowland Fells to the south now open up considerably and lead to some interesting speculation as to which cleft the Trough road goes through.

Continue 200 yards to a stile in the fence corner. The character of the walking now changes. It becomes wetter and rougher, and the sense of isolation grows despite the guiding fence and wall. Having crossed the stile follow the fence over the gently rising ground to a wall and cross the stile there. The route now follows a fence or wall for about $1^1/_2$ miles before it turns right to cut down to the stream, Tarnbrook Wyre.

The area between the fence and the waterfall in the main stream below is the site of a large gullery from May to mid August. Thousands and thousands of birds raise their broods there and fill the air with their raucous cries. When the chicks are hatched they make their presence felt with dive bombing attacks if you are too near. At one time some 500,000 birds nested there but their numbers have been reduced by culling in June as they became a danger to public health because of their insanitary feeding habits on domestic rubbish dumps - and Tarnbrook Wyre is part of our water supply.

You are at liberty to walk on either side of the boundary, but there's little between them. The fence/wall combination makes a great curve round the headwaters of the stream and the problem is knowing where to leave the fence, for this stretch has lengths of bare trackless peat and it is not easy to know just where you are. First and foremost ignore the large cairn well away to the right. It is a relic of the early days of grouse shooting on these moors before beaters were controlled by walkie-talkies. Wolfhole Crag with its rocky crest gets much nearer but that is not much help. However, the second ladder stile over the fence is at the right place. A small cairn and a yellow topped pole on the right confirm the place and you will soon find a well marked stony track. This leads you to the stream which you cross, possibly with some difficulty in wet weather. Just beyond it there is a sheltering rock outcrop where there was an open shed until quite recently.

In the days before the Land Rover, shooting parties rode up the hill by pony and this shed was the pony stables. Traces of the green pony track remain but it's the wide stony waterworks track that you use to descend to the tarmac road at Tarnbrook.

From Tarnbrook to Top of Emmetts

NOTE. If you do this walk in the short days of autumn or winter it is advisable to have two hours of GOOD light to get back to the Tower by the field paths described here. Otherwise return by the road, dull but not too dreary for if you finish in the dark the lights of the whole of Lancashire around Morecambe Bay twinkle and glow in a marvellous pattern at your feet.

Turn right on the tarmac road and walk through the little hamlet of Tarnbrook for about 100 yards. Just beyond a gateway there is a large triangular area of grass on the right. Opposite there is a barn on a short walled lane. This is the start of the return through the fields and it can be identified beyond doubt by the big pine tree. Almost all are waymarked with a discreet yellow arrow, a big help. Beyond the gate there is a good bridge over the Tarnbrook Wyre.

Tarnbrook

(Note that this bridge is marked ford on Map No.659.) Cross it and turn right to cross a white painted ladder stile. The next ladder stile can be seen ahead almost at once. Once across the muddy lane follow the hedge to the barn seen ahead then bear diagonally right to find the correct stile. Cross the wide ditch then follow the fence to the corner. NOW KEEP STRAIGHT ON to find the stile in the trees. Do a quick left then right and follow the far side of the hedge to Top of Emmetts on the Trough road.

Top of Emmetts to Meeting House Farm

Turn right and keep on the road, unpleasantly busy on a fine Sunday afternoon. You will pass the road junction to Abbeystead and then drop down a steep hill and pass the hamlet of Lower Lea at the junction of the road to Tarnbrook. As soon as you have crossed the River Grisedale, quite a small river, a gated farm track starts in a recess. Your stile is in the far wall of this recess and again it is waymarked. Despite this, finding the next stile, out of sight across this large field, is not easy. Follow the line of the wall past the line of trees that passes for a fence then bear right up the hillside aiming well to the left of the barn. When you are up this first slope the ground levels out and you should see the ladder stile away to your left.

Follow the fence through a large hayfield passing a collapsed old stile. Continue to a stile on the left that allows you to change sides of the fence, then after 50 yards or so cut across the field to the top of the wood to find a cart-track at a gate. Continue along it to a gate onto a lane. Turn right and almost opposite the farmhouse there is a not very obvious stile into the field. Follow the path in a direct line to Chapel House Farm ahead. Bear diagonally right to the corner of the hedge then to the gate into a large field. Pass over its crown and then head for the gate. Now head directly for Meeting House Farm ahead, so called because at one time there was a Quaker Meeting House here. See Walk 3.1 for something about it.

Meeting House Farm to Jubilee Tower

Continue along the access road to a right-hand corner then go through a snicket gate straight ahead. (At this point, if the light is fading it is better to stay on the road. It takes you first to Abbeystead lane in about 25 minutes then, having turned left, to the Trough Road and the Tower in about another 30 minutes.) Keep on the left-hand side of a poor row of trees that passes for a hedge, go through the corner of the next field then keep on the left of the fence or hedge through several fields mostly with gates not stiles to reach Lower Moor Head a short mile away. A stone step stile leads through their yard to the access road ahead. Here you may if the weather is kind, get a view once again of the Lake District Hills. Go straight across this road through a stile and continue the length of the field to find a very tight slit stile on the left of a decrepit gate. At the end of the next field change sides of the hedge by a not very obvious stile and continue in the same direction to reach Lee Tenement. Pass below the buildings into a short lane, turn right to reach Westfield House and continue up the wall side to the Tower and car park.

NICKY NOOK DIRECT FROM SCORTON   Walk 3.4

This short walk is one of the best in the book, combining a fine viewpoint with a return down a beautiful woodland valley.

Category:	C+
Time:	1¹⁄₂-2 hours
Distance:	2 miles
Map:	Pathfinder Series No.668 Garstang (SD44/54)
Start at:	Snowhill Lane, Scorton. It may be possible to park at the bottom of the lane opposite the post office. Failing that, there is room to park two or three cars just beyond the point where the lane crosses the M6.

Follow Snowhill Lane up the hill until it joins the road at the bottom of the fell, about a mile. The stile is opposite the junction and a well used, pleasant grassy path takes you up the hillside. Just after you have passed the wall beyond the little tarn, turn right and shortly bear left to continue this wide well used path to the trig point.

The views are extremely wide: nowhere does any nearby moor block the view. The fells are the view as you arrive with the shapely rounded domes of Bleasdale, Stake House and Harrisend Fells facing you. You should easily spot Blackpool Tower, and Fleetwood lies just to its right. Lancaster and Heysham are further right, the latter identified by its massive square built nuclear power station. Beyond them, the whale-backed mound of Black Combe is easily picked out.

When you have had your fill of the views, head towards the wall and take the right fork as you approach it, continuing to enjoy the splendid views of the Bowland Fells as you go down to the good stile into the lane. Turn right here and follow the cart-track, very wet in places, right down this delightful valley full of flowers in springtime, until you come to a gate and stile with a signpost which directs you to the right to return to Scorton. Follow the path up the side of the wood to reach the road where you turn right, and, after about 5 minutes, left down Tithe Barn lane to reach Scorton close to the church.

GRISE DALE AND HARRISEND FELL   Walk 3.5

This walk starts up the beautiful wooded valley of Grise Dale and continues along the foot of Harrisend Fell which has splendid views of the Lakes given a good day. It returns through the lower pastures, pleasant if not exciting walking. The viewpoint of Nicky Nook is an optional extra.

Category:	B
Time:	3¹/₂-4 hours
Distance:	8 miles
Maps:	Pathfinder Series No.668 Garstang and No.659 Galgate and Dolphinholme (SD44/54, SD45/55)
Start at:	Scorton Post Office. Scorton is best approached from the A6 at Cabus along the road signed the Trough of Bowland. There is very little parking in Scorton, and it is often full. Alternatively, you can start this walk at the very entrance to Grise Dale where there are a few places where you can get a car off the road just beyond the gate which gives access to the valley. This, unfortunately leaves you a long return on the road, but at least you can break it in Scorton at the cafe which you pass.

From the post office go along the Garstang road to the end of the village then turn left under the motorway. Continue up Tithe Barn Lane to a T-junction, turn right, and in about ¹/₄ mile just beyond a biggish house on the right, you will see a gate with stile on the left. Go down by the wood to join the path by the stream, turn left and enter Grise Dale, a wooded valley of great beauty in springtime.

Bluebells abound: the air is heavy with the scent of hawthorn and there is a good view of Nicky Nook, the most westerly outlier of the Bowlands looking far more imposing than its modest height of 215m. The excellent track continues the whole length of the valley passing the deep cut reservoir. There is a sharp bend on the track about half way along the reservoir and just beyond it a well built stone step stile enables you to go up the hillock of Nicky Nook - it is scarcely more than that - though it has a trig point. This modest climb (15 minutes) is a marvellous view point for the nearby Bowland Fells, the Lancashire coastal plain and the southern Lakeland Fells. From the stile a well trodden path leads first to a square stone tower of waterworks origin then a much fainter path continues to the trig point.

The view is wide, with the Fylde at your feet. You should easily spot Blackpool Tower and Fleetwood lies just to its right. Lancaster and Heysham are further right, the latter identified by its massive square built nuclear power station. Beyond them, the whale-backed mound of Black Combe is easily picked out, and if the day is really clear you may even make out the hills of Snowdonia some 60 or 70 miles away. Turning round, the

Bowland fells make a bigger visual impact than perhaps from any other viewpoint. They are close, they are big, though their rounded outlines mask their true size and lend an air of mystery, of things awaiting discovery.

Instead of retracing your steps all the way you will see a good wooden ladder stile to the left of your ascent path. Cross it and keep straight down the long field to find a stile into the wood that puts you onto the main cart-track through the valley close to a metal bridge. (If you haven't taken up the option of climbing Nicky Nook, continuing along the track by the reservoir will bring you to this bridge.) Turn left on the cart-track and follow it to the tarmacked road where you turn right to reach Fell End Farm. Turn right opposite the house going through the stockyard onto a cart-track and follow it up the field. Almost at the top there is a locked waterworks type of gate but the stile there has decayed and vanished. Cross over without much difficulty and continue to the gate at the top of the field. Continue to a second gate where the track is plainer, bear left to cross a tiny stream and follow a rough path to the road. Turn left and walk along the road for about a mile to the start of the path that runs across the foot of Harrisend Fell. It is marked by a finger post and little board announcing that it is the work of the Borough of Fylde County Services Management Board. (You can in fact reach this point direct from Fell End Farm but the path has completely disappeared and the ground is exceedingly rough and tussocky - and you need to hit off the correct point on the road. To do this, bear left round the back of the farm passing the clump of trees and continue to the road. This direct route is out of character with the rest of this walk and is not recommended unless you are used to that sort of rough going.)

The path across Harrisend Fell undulates and splits at times into sheep tracks but there are always poles to keep you on the right line so there are no real problems, and glorious views of the Lake District Fells. You must keep a lookout for the point where you turn left off this path to reach the track close to Lane Head as the poles continue. At a clump of rowan trees close to the corner of a newish fence turn left and follow a tiny track down Foxhouse Brook. You will join a farm road at a bend where you turn left, then at the next fence go over a broken stile on the left, follow the hedge down to another stile and the stream, crossed with the aid of one large stepping stone.

Turn right at the farm ahead and follow its access road to the public road.

Turn left and in a few yards turn right through a gate into a field. Climb steadily over the crown of the hill then pass to the right of the isolated trees making for the middle one of three buildings to find the stile onto the road. Turn left, then right into the yard of the joiner's shop and through the gate at its end into the field. Follow the hedge on the left to the stile then cut down the field to reach Salisbury Farm by a little footbridge. Go right through the farmyard, over another bridge and up the field to a pair of white gate posts which you pass through. Continue to the far corner of the wood to the stile then follow the hedge to reach the access road to the gravel quarry. Straight across another pair of stiles take you through a narrow band of woodland then follow the fence down the hillside into a narrow track, often very muddy. This will bring you to a stile on the left which you cross. (Note that the path across the gravel pit workings to this point is a diversion not shown on the OS map). Follow the side of the wood, pleasantly poised above Foxhouse Brook, then across the field to reach Foxhouse Farm. Go straight through the farmyard onto their access road where you turn left. In the bend of the road ahead turn right into a lane and at the first gate on the right get into the field by some means or other. (The gate is collapsed and wired up but there are other ways.) Pass the pile of stones on its left, then a pond on its right, and bear left to follow first the stream then the wood to the remains of a stile onto the road. Turn left on the road and follow it into Scorton, a short mile.

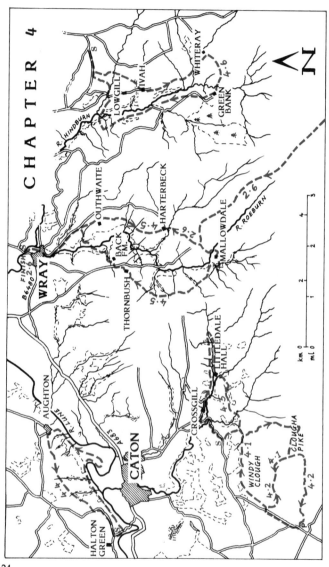

N

R HINDBURN

LOWGILL

IVAH

WHITERAY

GREEN BANK

4·6

OUTHWAITE

HARTERBECK

BACK PACK

5·4

2·6

MALLOWDALE

R ROEBURN

2·6

WRAY

FINISH
B6480 2·6

THORNBUSH

5·4

km 0   1   2   3   4
ml 0   1   2   3

AUGHTON

R LUNE

A683

CATON

CROSSGILL

LITTLEDALE HALL

4·5

S

WINDY CLOUGH

4·2

4·1

1

CLOUGHA PIKE

4·2

P

HALTON GREEN

Chapter 4

WALKS AROUND THE NORTHERN FRINGE

Climbing Clougha Pike

4.1   Clougha Pike from Little Cragg car park, Category B
4.2   Clougha Pike from Birk Bank car park, Category B

Other Walks

4.3   A short walk up Littledale, Category C
4.4   Up the River Lune from Caton Bridge to Aughton, Category B
4.5   The Headwaters of the River Hindburn, Category B+
4.6   Around the head of Roeburndale, Category B+

The title of this chapter is intended to suggest its scattered nature, though these walks have one thing in common: their streams all drain into one or another tributary of the Lune, indeed, one of the walks, No.4.4, lies principally along the Lune itself, returning along the higher land to the north of the valley which, for some odd reason, is included in the Forest of Bowland Area of Outstanding Natural Beauty.

CLIMBING CLOUGHA PIKE

Clougha is the abrupt end of the north-west lobe of the Bowlands moors, its rough rocky escarpment standing boldly above Lancaster. Its highest point is Clougha Pike, a modest 413m (1,355ft) high and an absolutely superb view point on a good day. The Clougha Access Area is part of the larger of the two Access Areas in the Bowlands and from it an Access Strip runs over Grit Fell and Ward's Stone to Tarnbrook. It has a number of paths not shown on the OS map.

The Area has three car parks giving access to various sides of it and four routes to the top of Clougha Pike. The one from Jubilee Tower can be dismissed as of little consequence. The right of way track from near Quernmore Post Office is but a second best but valuable as it is not subject to closure on the days when shooting is in

Grit Fell and Ward's Stone from Little Cragg car park

progress as the other routes are. The real little gems are from Birk Bank and Little Cragg car parks, in fact the walk from the latter is arguably the best short moorland walk in the Bowlands.

CLOUGHA PIKE FROM LITTLE CRAGG CAR PARK   Walk 4.1

This walk uses a rather circuitous approach on the flanks of Littledale to a point midway between Grit Fell and Clougha Pike that is close to the cairns of the Three Chairs and descends from the Pike almost to Birk Bank car park from where it returns to Little Cragg across the lower slopes of the Access Area. The path splits and becomes faint on the upper part of the outward leg of the walk and some route finding ability is needed. Given a clear day the views are unsurpassed and there is a wide and interesting variety of terrain on the descent.

Category:	B
Time:	3½ -4 hours
Distance:	6½ miles
Maps:	Pathfinder Series No.637 Burton-in-Kendal and No.659 Galgate and Dolphinholme (SD56/57 and SD45/55). Note that the paths used are shown as faint dashed lines, not the green of right of way tracks.

Start at: Little Cragg car park. This is just to the right of the words Little
            Cragg on the OS map and is a pair of gravelled roadside areas at
            almost the highest point of the Littledale-Quernmore road. It is
            probably best approached from junction 34 of the M6, taking the
            A683 to Caton. Turn right here between the Station Hotel and a
            garage - it is signed Littledale - then turn left after about a mile,
            again signed Littledale, and bear right to Brookhouse. Follow this
            road for a couple of miles to a junction at New House Farm and turn
            right here, signed Quernmore. Then climb steeply up the hill to the
            car parking area just beyond the gate at the farm.
            Alternatively, if you are coming from East Lancashire, travel via
            Clitheroe, Dunsop Bridge and the Trough of Bowland road to
            Quernmore village crossroads, turn right there, turn right again in $^1/_2$
            mile, and yet again turn right after about 1$^1/_2$ miles. The car parking
            area is about 1$^1/_2$ miles further on.

Little Cragg to Clougha Pike

Assuming you have used the approach given above, walk back up the
road to the cattle grid and go right to a stile. From it a green cart-track
leads you down the field, passes a small barn on its right then curves
to the left to a decrepit gate. Continue up the field to Skelbow barn,
named on the map. Turn left in front of the barn and follow the track
to the end of the wall and then turn sharp right following the pleasant
green cart-track up the side of the wood until you reach a stile into the
Access Area.

Cross the stile and turn right towards the wide green track that
climbs the hill. Just before you get to the stream, the infant River
Conder, in less than 100 yards, a hollow green track goes up the hill
on the left. Follow its easily graded curves up the steep bit of the
hillside and as the ground flattens out, the good track disappears.
However it is replaced by a rather faint path and a few small cairns
and leads to a fairly obvious slanting track crossing the hillside to the
left. Follow this for some considerable distance and where it
degenerates to a much smaller track and forks, take the right-hand
one. This continues in much the same direction until you come in
sight of a notice board which says, "Limit of Access Land". Now the
track improves and tends to run directly up the fellside passing a long
line of old shooting butts. At their end the gradient eases. The track
now starts to bend to the right and reaches a great saucer like hollow

in the fellside where it becomes faint and splits up in the midst of knolls of heather and rock outcrops. Take a left fork just beyond a small solitary marker stone and follow it bearing left across the hollow to arrive at the Three Chairs on the broad ridge that connects Clougha with Grit Fell. Turn right and ten minutes sees you at the trig point on Clougha Pike with its capacious shelter-wall and marvellously wide views over the Bay.

Far away to the left Morecambe Bay ends in effect at Fleetwood. You may even see Blackpool Tower to its left. Then let your eye travel to the right. There is a stretch of coast without any distinguishing features until you come to the Lune Estuary. If the tide is in a sinuous finger of water stretches right into the heart of Lancaster, a reminder that in the eighteenth century Lancaster was a major port trading with America and the West Indies. The city lies at your feet easily picked out by the green dome of the Ashton Memorial. Heysham, with its nuclear power station and docks, is behind it to the left, then comes Morecambe itself. Beyond Morecambe, across the wide curve of the bay, lies Grange-over-Sands with the Lake District hills as a back cloth. To the left of them is the hump of Black Combe and further left still on an incredibly long strip of land is Walney Island and Barrow-in-Furness. Whether the tide is in or not the sands are always wet and the Bay is a subtle pattern of shades of blue, sometimes glittering, sometimes merging quietly to grey or to brown and sometimes splashed with brilliant streaks of light. It is magnificent.

Clougha Pike to Birk Bank

Leave the trig point along the northern escarpment, Clougha Scar, aiming for a large heap of stones a few hundred yards away. The track tends to split: keep well over to the edge to be sure of finding the end of a wall where you scramble down a big gritstone block or two and continue under a slightly lower tier of rocks until you come to a stile.

Carry on straight ahead and follow the wide but vague track as it swings back to the right about 100 yards above a stile at the end of Little Windy Clough. A good track continues through pleasant woodland, sessile oak, birch and rowan, our native British hardwoods, and in due course reaches a stile on the edge of a big area of sedges, reeds and rushes. You cross this dry shod on duckboards - without them you would probably be waist deep - and at the other side emerge onto a wide grassy cart-track. Turn right here and in a few yards there is a left fork which would take you to Birk Bank car park,

New bridge over the River Roeburn near Wray
Whitray Beck

Harterbeck Bridge
The river at Grindleton

only 200 yards away. However, you keep straight on.

Birk Bank to Little Cragg

This excellent green track runs amongst bracken and heather along a low ridge at the foot of the last bit of rocky ground for a good ¹/₂ mile. It gives delightful easy walking with views across the valley, the valley of the River Conder which flows into the Lune at Glasson Dock. When the woodland on your right is ending take the left fork passing a square stone pillar with odd looking square grooves in it. Continue as before, crossing a deep cut stream bed by an unusually large bridge, Ottergear Bridge. A North West Water notice informs you that the bridge is not a right of way and may be closed at any time without notice. Well, you wouldn't be stuck, the ravine can be crossed without the bridge. Presumably this bridge carries a water main, indeed, it seems likely that the path owes its existence to water works activity. Beyond the bridge the track (which is no longer shown on the OS map) gradually drops towards the wall passing a 'no access' gate and continuing to a stile and gate. Here it is possible to leave the access area and cut about ¹/₂ hour off the time required to return. Simply go down to the farm and onto the road, turn right and plod on to the car park, uphill all the way.

Assuming you are going to finish the job properly continue along the cart-track that leaves the gate and works its way up the rough ground eventually entering a little ravine, the upper part of the stream you crossed a little earlier. Cross the wall by the stile, continue up the steadily climbing path to the shoulder where this broad path turns right and climbs up the fellside. A much smaller one leaves it on the left and this is the way you go. This path is very narrow yet always well defined. It undulates along the fell at this level for about ¹/₂ mile until it comes to the top of some woodland then drops down into the valley below. It now continues up this valley, broken and faint in places, and crossing a sizeable stream until it reaches the stile on the left where you leave the Access Area. Now simply retrace your steps to the car park.

CLOUGHA PIKE FROM BIRK BANK CAR PARK   Walk 4.2

This walk uses the obvious way up Clougha Pike from Birk Bank car park, is well trodden and straightforward but covers some rough ground. It returns to the road close to Quernmore Post Office by the right of way paths through the rough pastures by Rowten Brook, and returns to the car park by a sizeable chunk of road. The ascent route is used for descent by the previous walk.

Category:	B
Time:	2 hours
Distance:	3½ miles
Maps:	Pathfinder Series No.637 Burton-in-Kendal and No.659 Galgate and Dolphinholme (SD56/57 and SD45/55). The paths used on the ascent are shown as faint dashed lines, but that for descent is shown in the customary green of right of way tracks.
Start at:	Birk Bank car park. On Pathfinder map No.637 this car park is where the letters CP of Quernmore CP are located and it is passed when following the instructions given in Walk 4.1 previously if arriving from the M6 Junction 33 or from East Lancashire. If coming from Junction 37 to Little Cragg, continue to a left turn, take it and you will reach it in about a mile.

Leave the car park by the gate at the back corner and follow the wide green track for about 200 yards to a first fork. Turn right and follow this to another wide green track where you turn right again. A stile on the left of a locked gate puts you onto a long length of duckboards that sees you safely across a big area of reeds and rushes to another stile. Then climb steadily up through woodland, oak, birch and rowan, our native hardwoods, growing through gorse, heather and bilberry, typical of high level Pennine woodland. A well trodden path leads you to two stiles close together. Use the right-hand one. (The left-hand one leads into Windy Clough and the Pike by a more circuitous route, neither well trodden nor easy to follow.) Continue very steeply up the field and follow the wall round the field to a gate. The path continues to the right below a tier of rocks and climbs gently up to reach a wall. Turn right and follow it to its end abutting onto a massive gritstone block. Scramble up a couple of blocks of gritstone and continue along the upper escarpment to the trig point and capacious shelter-wall on the summit. See the previous walk for a description of the view.

Descent by the Right of Way Path

When you have soaked up that magnificent view leave by a not very obvious track on the other side of the shelter wall. It will become quite clear after a few yards and drops comfortably down the steep upper slopes and then leads across to the stream which it crosses. Animal tracks confuse it in several places, simply keep from 50 to 100 yards from the wall to your right. Head down the rough pastures to the Access gate (you are now leaving the Access Area) go through the right-hand one of two gates ahead then go straight down the cart-track to Rooten Brook Farm. Bear right between the farm buildings to its tarmac access road. Continue down this, cross the stream again and in 50 yards you will see a large green painted shed. Immediately before it go into the walled green lane that runs down the side of the wood emerging in a field just above a house in a distinctive hollow. Make for the wall corner to the right, follow the wall to the gate into the property, then follow their access road to the public road. Turn right on the road and it is a 15 minute plod back to the car park. Take care to take the right fork after about 5 minutes. If the day and the time is right you may care first of all to turn left and have an ice cream at Quernmore Post Office, just about 5 minutes away to the left.

OTHER WALKS

A SHORT WALK UP LITTLEDALE   Walk 4.3

Riverside right of way paths are all too scarce in Bowland and this one could hardly be more beautiful in springtime. Though it is just possible to park at the start of the bridleway up the valley it is not recommended and the walk perforce starts at Little Cragg car park and uses the road to reach the start of the bridleway. This has been waymarked all the way to the road that leads into the head of Roeburndale from Caton, but the walk does not go as far as that. Instead it returns down the valley by the side of the stream then climbs out of it close to Littledale Hall and returns along the foot of the fells to Little Cragg car park. Several major streams are crossed but all have good bridges so the walk is very suitable for a bad day or it could be done on the same day as one of the walks over Clougha (4.1 or 4.2).

Category:	C
Time:	2 hours
Map:	Pathfinder Series No.637 Burton-in Kendal (SD56/57)

Start at: Little Cragg car park. See Walk 4.1 for instructions.

Walk down the steep road which has good views as far as New House Farm and turn right there. Continue through the hamlet of Crossgill, passing first the entrance to Littledale Hall, then the former chapel, a curious building dated 1752 and now a house. A grassy cart-track leaves the sharp corner of the road ahead and you turn into it. At first it goes through woodland then, to your amazement, an isolated church appears ahead.

In fact it is no longer a church but winter quarters for sheep. Beyond it you get your first views of Littledale, a deep cut and well wooded valley with the fells rising grandly behind. If there are no leaves on the trees you will get glimpses of Littledale Hall, no ancient pile but an impressive collection of Victorian buildings. They were built by John Dodson, who was Vicar of Cockerham and the son of a wealthy Liverpool shipping family, probably between 1840 and 1850. He also built the church in 1849 and is buried, together with some of his family, in the vault behind the church. Despite its surrounding fence, one of the inscribed stones has been smashed.

At the end of a wall the track forks, the right-hand one going down to the Hall and the left continuing up the valley. Take the left-hand one and after ¹/₂ mile or so, stay below the fence when it goes into a field. Now go through the top of a length of the woodland and on emerging, cross a small stream and climb steeply up for about 20 yards. The path now continues along a broad green track neatly poised above the river for almost ¹/₂ mile enjoying the fine views of the valley. Eventually it fizzles out and you drop down to a ford and a ruined bridge. Return along a lower track which is often very wet, and follows the banks of the stream. It enters the woods just above Littledale Hall where there is a pond and you may see traces of a weir in the river, relics, probably, of a former mill. All too soon you will find yourself looking across at the back of Littledale Hall and its attendant buildings.

Cross the bridge leading to the Hall, turn left and go past a nondescript building where fans hum incessantly.

This is the heart of a complex of buildings that produce eggs for hatching on a vast scale, and the chicks that become the hens that lay your breakfast eggs are reared there.

At its end continue through the complex of buildings and turn right through a little gate at their end. A good track takes you into the

Littledale Hall

woods again and to the bridge over Foxdale Beck. Shortly after crossing the bridge the track makes a sharp bend to the right and zigzags up through the wood to emerge into a rough field. Go straight ahead to the wall corner to find a fine stone step stile that takes you to Field Head, one of many remote farms in Bowland perched on the very highest of the pastures. Cut across to their access road and follow it to Bell Hill Farm. It's an open bit of road, exposed to the weather but with fine views both to the fells on the left which now seem very close and over Morecambe Bay.

Go through the gate at Bell Hill and turn left in the yard following a good track down to the ford and footbridge over Uldale Beck, a spot with a "touch of the wild" about its rushing waters on a bad day, delightful in summer. Continue up the field to a gate into the wood where you pick up a good cart-track that takes you right to Skelbow Barn, even named on the map. Go through the right-hand gate here, finding a grassy cart-track that goes down a long field, takes you through a gate on the left, passes a small barn and climbs up to the road at a cattle grid. Little Cragg car park is on your left.

UP THE RIVER LUNE FROM CATON BRIDGE TO AUGHTON
Walk 4.4

The River Lune upstream from Caton Bridge is without doubt one of its finest lengths and this walk follows it as far as Aughton Barns. It then climbs out of the valley and returns through the fields on the high ground to Halton Park from where it takes the road back to the bridge. The field paths for the return are little used and some care is needed in route finding.

Category:	B
Time:	3 hours, possibly more if route finding proves difficult
Map:	Pathfinder Series No.637 Burton-in Kendal (SD56/57)
Start at:	Caton Bridge picnic site. It is not marked on the OS map but is well signed from the A683 Lancaster to Kirkby Lonsdale Road.

Leave the picnic site by the wide track down to the river and turn left into the woods at the finger post. You are now on the Lune Valley Way and you follow it upstream, making the most of its good stiles and bridges.

Almost at once there is a fine view of Ingleborough which you will enjoy the whole way along the river, and shortly Caton Low Mill comes into view across the river. This substantial building was erected in 1783 as a cotton spinning mill, receiving its raw cotton by the bale from the Port of Lancaster which was even then importing cotton from America. As was normal in those times its labour force was mainly pauper children, brought from the big cities and housed communally. Originally water powered, it was modernised and ran until 1970, an unusually long life for an early cotton mill.

You will drop down to the very water's edge as you arrive at the wood but almost at once climb up a little and continue through the wood, a tangle of scrub blackberry in autumn. In the next length of field you will see a "bridge", which turns out to be part of the Thirlmere Aqueduct when you get closer. Pass under it and enter the next length of wood again keeping to the higher path. Towards the end it is steep and full of tree roots and needs a bit of care. Now you rejoin the river bank itself and follow it for a couple of miles or so to Aughton Barns, diverting briefly as follows. After a mile or so when you have almost completed the great horseshoe loop of river you will see a large barn in good condition on the left. Cut across to it and follow the fence then the higher ground away from the river gradually veering right to rejoin the river bank where it is reinforced with stone.

Along this length of river, you are likely to see fishermen, often waist deep in the water, whipping yards and yards and yards of fine nylon line through the air as they cast the fly for salmon, for the Lune is famous for its salmon. They "run" from the sea to their spawning grounds in the autumn and are fished from February to October, some times with fly, sometimes with worm, sometimes with a metal spinner depending on the amount of water in the river. These great sporting fish may weigh as much as 20lbs.

At Aughton Barns you will find a cart-track that takes you past the house and becomes a road as it climbs steeply up the hill to Aughton, a hamlet perched on the upper slopes of the Lune valley. Go straight across the little crossroads and 200 yards higher up you will see a fingerpost in the hedge on the left, the start of the return footpaths. Bear left across the end of a hedge to find the stile and continue in the same direction to find the next one, a distinctive iron ladder stile. Now make towards the left-hand end of the farm, Far Highfield, then to the hedge corner ahead. Now follow the hedge (passing two redundant stiles where field boundaries have been changed) to Middle Highfield.

As you top the rise you will get a glimpse of Morecambe Bay and the Williamson Memorial to the left, and on a really good day, a break in the hedge gives you a view to the Lakes, with the Langdale Pikes easily identified but dwarfed by the mass of Bowfell to their left.

Getting through the farmyard at Middle Highfield is complicated. Immediately after the first house go to the left through a good metal gate, bear right towards the chapel-like house to find a stone stile to pass it, turn left at the end of its garden to reach the field where it is apt to be pretty filthy, and bear right to find the first stile. Now continue to the right towards a very substantial stone wall and follow it to the field corner. Here a semi derelict unopenable gate awaits you: do the best you can, then go through the gate almost opposite. Go down the hedge side on the right towards Lower Highfield and continue across the bottom of the field to reach the gate in the far corner. Then go left before you reach the house, through a sort of farmyard and two more gates to cross the access road and reach a little stream, easily crossed. Once through the gate ahead aim for the right-hand end of the wood where you will find a small swing gate into it. The surprisingly well trodden path runs just inside the fence at first then continues in a straight line through the wood and the next field to reach the hedge corner. Now simply follow the hedge to a stile with a white arrow on it and then into the field. This keeps you out of the complex of buildings around Halton Park. Meanwhile there are splendid views of the whole of the Lune valley and the fells beyond

Caton: from right to left, Clougha, Grit Fell and Wards Stone. Continue in the field for about 100 yards and when you have passed a large shed, immediately turn left to find the stile on to a gravel road. Turn right and follow it to the tarmac road where you turn left into Park Lane. Now simply follow this road, which has little traffic and good views, to a T-junction, turn left and continue to the picnic site.

Warning

The disused length of railway line in the Lune valley has been converted into a walking route which is easily reached from the Caton picnic site. It leads to Bull Beck car park and picnic site, though as it is enclosed by scrub trees and lacks views it is not very interesting. The bank of the Lune is also easily reached from Bull Beck, but families who think that a pleasant short circular walk can be made between the two car parks should be aware that there is no bridge across Artle Beck which is a large stream, not usually crossable without wellies.

THE HEADWATERS OF THE RIVER HINDBURN   Walk 4.5

In some ways this is a companion walk to No.4.6 crossing the many brooks and gills that drain the fells. All river crossings have good bridges. Despite the upstream and downstream routes being less than a mile apart they have considerable differences in character. The outward one crosses the wide open pastures and rough grazing, the return one drops into the well wooded valley of the Hindburn and gives a fine length of riverside walking before climbing steadily back to the car. Both have excellent and very different views.

Category:	B+
Time:	5 hours, more if you have route finding problems. Attention to the text and good map reading are required.
Distance:	9 miles
Map:	Pathfinder Series No.650 High Bentham and Clapham (SD66/76) is indispensable.
Start at:	the cattle grid on Aikengill Road which leaves the High Bentham to Slaidburn road on the right 2 miles above High Bentham. There is room to get a car off the road.

The Cattle Grid to Whitray

Cross the cattle grid and continue down the road for 5-7 minutes to the first lane on the left. Follow this to its end at Foss Bank Farm, go straight through the farmyard into the field and down to the stream, then cross the footbridge. Tread delicately along the very edge of the stream and immediately before you turn sharp left up the bank, spare a glance to the right when you will see how the farm gets its name, for the side stream has a fine little waterfall - the foss, a word of Scandinavian origin. Continue up the next two fields to arrive at the back of Brackenbottom. Turn right to pass behind the buildings then go straight across the end of the yard and through the left-hand one of two gates. The stile is in the wall to the right. Now follow the wall to the slight bend, then follow the ditch down to find the bridge over Bull Gill. Climb steeply up a little to the left to find the stile out of the gill, then follow the fence direct to the road crossing one stile on the way. Turn left and continue up the hill to the hamlet of Ivah where you continue by the Botton Head road.

After a couple of wriggles in the road there is a short straight bit then a sharp right-hand corner. At this corner turn left into the access road that leads to Swans.

Here you are on the line of the Roman road that crossed the Bowland Fells on its way from Ribchester to Low Burrowbridge, as indeed you have been since you joined the road just before the hamlet. A glance at the OS map will show you its line across country. At this point nothing is visible of it, but traces of it will be seen a little later in this walk.

At Swans pass between the house and the barn and turn left where the tractor track goes through the gate. Continue along the line of the old hedge/fence following a faint green bridle track to Williamson's Gill, enjoying fine views of the fells ahead, White Hill to the left and Wolfhole Crag well to the right. Cross the gill by a stone bridge, then struggle under the wire netting that replaces a small damaged gate. Hopefully this will have been replaced by the time you read this. Ahead you will see a length of wall with a stile and gate, but this is NOT YOUR ROUTE, and it is crucial that you bear diagonally left to find a gateway that is out of sight, then continue in the same direction down this large field to locate the hidden stone slit stile in a slight bend of the left-hand field boundary and below it, a good footbridge over Whitray Beck, a fine place for lunch. Now head steeply up the field aiming at the wall corner then go straight to the farm and through the yard onto the road.

Whitray Head to Stairend Bridge

Turn right and follow the road to its end at Dickinson's, passing Botton Head with its date stone of 1666. The style of the house is not nearly so old as that and the stone may have been taken from an earlier house. Just as you enter the farmyard go through a gate on the right and go down to the stream, the infant River Hindburn, adjusting your course to Holmes Barn, a large decrepit building, as soon as you see it.

You cross the line of the Roman road as you go down this field. It is best located by looking to the fell on the left where you will see the line of the road as an unmistakable pale line running down the nose of the fell. When you are in line with it look for a shallow ridge where the grass is somewhat yellower than the rest of this green field. It's got to be admitted that it needs a little imagination and the right conditions to see it, but it can be seen very convincingly both here and across the moor to its right as you climb the hillside opposite.

Cross the bridge and follow the fence on the right up the hillside, though the start is so steep you will inevitably divert a little to the left, and go through the first gate on the right. Continue up the field following, bearing right below Lower Green Bank and continue down the field to the gate which you go through. Carry on across the field dropping down a little to find a good stone step stile, then drop down towards the buildings to pick up a stony cart-track and follow it to the road. Turn right and in less than 1/2 mile turn right into the short access road to Lower Thrushgill.

Now is the time to appreciate the fine views of the Yorkshire Dales peaks across the valley, the unmistakable Ingleborough on the right, to its left Whernside showing a bolder profile than usual, then Gragareth backed up by Crag Hill.

Go to the left of the farmhouse which has a datestone 1798, through a little gate and continue in a dead straight line towards the ruins of Lower House Barn. The first gate is quite obvious, the next stile is a mere apology for one on the down side of the hedge but the last one is a good stone step stile. Keep going in the same direction to reach a line of trees which are the remains of an old hedge, and at their end drop down to a gate on the road at Stairend Bridge.

Stairend Bridge to Aitkengill Road

Turn left and at the sharp bend of the road just ahead go through a gate into a very pleasant riverside field, the start of a first class stretch of riverside and woodland walking. Stay on this wide lower part following a cart/tractor-track besides the river bank to a gate. It then climbs up onto a sort of level and disappears, just when you need guidance most.

Keep on this level until you can see the ruins of a building ahead and above then head up to it. You will probably find that cart-track again. Go through the gate beyond and keeping on this level thread a way through the many humps and bumps in this field, the remains of some ancient landslide, and head for the wood where you will find a gate through to the field. Follow a faint green cart-track up the field to another ruin, then continue through two fields at this level. Ahead you will see a tree filled ravine. Cut across to it and follow its fence down to the stile. Across this, miraculously it would seem, a well trodden little path appears and takes you through the wood and to the footbridge over the River Hindburn.

Turn left to find another path climbing out of the valley by a set of huge steps, suitable only for a six foot man.

These steps, known locally as Fairy Steps, were rebuilt by members of the local community at the request of the Parish Council and organised by the Countryside Service. The local people were keen to have the exact number of steps that the original flight had had but made the flight a little bit longer, so the steps had to be higher.

At the stile head for the barn where you are on a cart-track, then in the second field leave it for the left-hand one of two gates. Now go straight ahead to reach the road just above Mill Bridge, Lowgill. Turn left, and as soon as you have crossed the bridge turn right onto the steep and narrow road to Lowgill Church.

Lowgill church serves the scattered parish of Tatham and its true name is the Tatham Fells Church of the Good Shepherd, a most appropriate name for a church in an area whose economy is dependent on sheep. The church is a simple but good Victorian structure with a central tower, built in 1885-7 by Paley and Austin, a well known firm of Lancaster church restorers, for £1,200. There had been a church on this site since 1577, possibly earlier.

It had fallen into decay by 1738, and had been restored in 1840. The population must have been flourishing in Victorian time s- the house at Whitray was built during that period.

Go into the churchyard, pass the church and at its end immediately turn right and go through a little gate surmounted by an iron arch. Turn left and follow a little path into the field. Head diagonally left towards the barn then continue up the field towards the house, Rantree Fold Farm. Go through the farmyard to reach the road, turn right, and 10 minutes sees you back to the cattle grid and your car.

AROUND THE HEAD OF ROEBURNDALE   Walk 4.6

There are no right of way paths up the River Roeburn's deep cut valley but a very fine walk can be made around its headwaters by means of the tracks that connect the remote moorland farms. It is a good deal more demanding than the map may lead you to expect. Three major tributaries valleys have to be crossed with considerable loss and re-gain of height - and you start off by throwing away a good deal of height to cross the Roeburn.

Category:	B+
Time:	5-5½ hours
Distance:	8 miles
Maps:	Pathfinder Series No.650 High Bentham and Clapham and No.637 Burton-in-Kendal and Caton (SD66/76, SD65/57)
Start at:	the track to Back Farm, Roeburndale West. This is most easily reached by turning as indicated at the Hornby crossroads on the B6480 rather than from Wray itself. The track starts about 2½ miles up the road and has a public footpath signpost. It is possible to park a car off the road just before the start of the track to the farm.

Back Farm to Harterbeck Farm

The route across the valley is waymarked all the way to the road on the other side, a considerable help. However, some guidance may not come amiss. At Back Farm go left along a vague grassy cart-track to the farm on the other side of the cleft that separates them. Turn right into the field at the gate, cut across to the left-hand fence and follow it until you come to a stile. From it a steep track with some steps leads down to a stile into a clearing where there is a new building close to some ruins. Continue ahead, and you will shortly come to a good cart-track where you turn right and then keep left until you see the Nature Trail sign. Follow the sign down to the new bridge.

It is about 100 yards below the site of the bridge that was washed away by that terrible flood of 1967. You will see a big steel girder now in two parts, lying just above the stones. It was one of the main supports of the bridge and was bent double after the flood, just as if it were a hairpin. It makes it easier to believe that a farmhouse across the river was demolished by the flood and the many stones strewn about the field are all that remain of it.

Follow the Nature Trail sign across the field and into the wood and continue along it as it climbs up and leaves the wood. (Note that the right of way path has been diverted and is not as shown on the map.) At the next gate go straight ahead across a wet place to a gate into a small field across which lies the road. NOW turn right at once to find the stile masked by a holly bush and then follow the hedge up the first field and the broad ditch cum stream up the second to the stile in the corner and the access road to Outhwaite Farm.

As you walk up the field look across the valley to the right. You will see a long straggly line of conifers with a cart-track by their side. This is where the walk ends, well, almost, at Thornbush.

Go almost straight across this road and follow the wall into a grassy walled lane. At its end go through the right-hand one of two gates and continue to follow the wall through a number of damp rushy fields, the haunt of the curlew and lapwing in early spring, for a mile or more.

As you drop over the first gentle rise you can just make out the three chimneys of Harterbeck in its band of sheltering trees. Behind stretches the long ridge of the Wyresdale Fells, from right to left Clougha, a barely distinguishable rise, then Grit Fell, Ward's Stone and finally, well to the left, Wolfhole Crag. In front of Ward's Stone stands Mallowdale Pike, identified by its conical shape.

When that guiding wall ends you will see a slit stile ahead. From it cut across to the wall corner and then to the barn where you will find a good gravel cart-track at the gate. Follow it for about 400 yards when you will see three gates in a row: go through the last one. Failure to do so is liable to land you in a muck heap worthy of the

141

Augean Stables! From the gate follow the fence almost to Harterbeck Farm but go through the gate on the left to avoid the stockyard.

Harterbeck Farm to High Salter

Cross the farm access road to follow a cart-track down to a ford and stone slab bridge over the little stream. When the cart-track swings left, follow the wall to pick up a lower green track that leads to a new bridge over the head of Pedder Ghyll.

The great flood of 1967 washed away the original bridge and it was not replaced until 1987. The family from Harterbeck used to come this way to the Methodist Chapel at Lower Salter every Sunday, but now the ubiquitous motor car takes over. The bridge is cupped in a sheltered green hollow with a crescent of sheep cropped turf by the stream, a superb picnic spot, whilst in dry weather the little stream merely tinkles over the waterfall.

From the bridge take the slightly higher rake of the two and as this steep shoulder levels out, start to cross this rough field diagonally right to a slit stile near the wall corner. Now continue up the field to reach a gate, bearing right to cross the ditch on a green bridge. Now go diagonally right across this large field to find a stile in the corner on the left of the gate. Cross this, bear right to follow the wall over the rise, and High Salter lies ahead just a field's length away.

High Salter to Winder

Turn left on the road, pass the farm buildings and you will see a finger post on the right. Mallowdale Farm is straight ahead, perched on a spur of the fell that juts out into the valley. Turn right passing the barns and follow the wall down the hillside to reach a gate onto a farm access road. Turn left and follow this road across the River Roeburn and up the hill to Mallowdale. Go between the house and the farm buildings and now you will see Haylot, like Mallowdale perched on a spur of the hill, and if you look across the valley and somewhat to the right, you will see Winder.

It's one of the unusual things about this walk, you can see your next objective from the previous one. You may marvel too, how people make a living in these remote upland farms. Presumably as "less favoured areas" they qualify for grants from the EEC.

When you get into the field beyond the farm bear left a little and go very steeply down a green bridleway to the bridge over Mallow

Gill, almost a gorge, and one of the choicer bits of the walk. Then follow the well marked path steeply up through the wood crossing the fence where the path ends, despite the lack of a proper stile. Now follow the fence to the right going round the top of the wood to the wall. Climb the stile then follow the other side of the wall to Haylot using the gate on the right to reach the road. Turn right at the farm gate then left onto a good farm access road only 50 yards or so away. This road, which crosses Bladderstone Back and climbs up to the Roeburndale Road, is not shown on the 1:25,000 map. Turn right at the junction and Winder is only 200 yards away.

Winder to Thornbush

Bear left at Winder making for the barn and note in passing a stone with the date 1677 in the back of the house. From the barn follow a cart-track, often cow churned and a bit filthy, into the fields beyond Crogley Gill Beck where there is a plantation on the left. Go through a gate and then leave the faint track striking diagonally right aiming somewhat above the top of the wood in Warm Beck. You should be opposite a brownish band of washed out earth where it is easy to cross the beck then climb straight up the field to find the stile in a length of damaged wall. The stile, however, is quite serviceable if not easily spotted. Go straight ahead but bearing slightly left and climbing gently, and when you see it, make for the corner of the fence. Hereabouts you will pick up a good gravel farm track. Follow it first to the straggly line of conifers mentioned earlier then down to Thornbush. Continue to the road, turn left and 5 minutes will see you back at your car.

Chapter 5
WALKS AROUND THE SOUTHERN FRINGE

Starting at Sawley
5.1 Sawley to Bolton-by-Bowland, Category B
5.2 The Ribble Way from Sawley, Category B
5.3 Easington Fell from Sawley, Category A or B+

Starting at Hurst Green
5.4 Longridge Fell and the Hodder, Category B+ or B

STARTING AT SAWLEY

SAWLEY TO BOLTON-BY-BOWLAND   Walk 5.1

The stile beyond the river bridge at Sawley somehow invites exploration of the countryside beyond, and this walk to Bolton-by-Bowland does just that. It is hardly a riverside walk but a walk through highly scenic parkland. After a stroll through the village the walk returns by a different route but involves fording Skirden Beck, not easy except in dry weather, though there is an acceptable alternative.

Category: B
Time: about 2½ hours plus time spent in the village
Distance: 6 miles, 7½ if you divert from the ford
Map: Pathfinder Series No.669 Chipping and Clitheroe (SD64/74)
Start at: Sawley. There is room to park three or four cars off the road on the
            north side of the Ribble bridge. Alternatively roadside parking is
            possible near the Spread Eagle and the Abbey ruins.

Go past the hotel and over the river bridge where you will find a little gate into the field on the right - and a notice instructing you to keep away from the river banks and follow the hedge. A later one instructs you to follow the white stones. It gives the feeling that you are not

CHAPTER 5

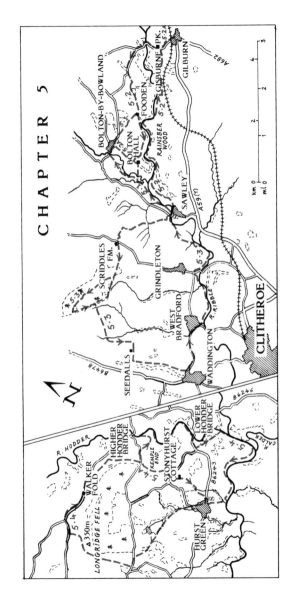

wanted here, but this is a right of way path and you are not to be denied its use. Do as you are bidden and in three field lengths you will reach the banks of the Ribble, if briefly. At the same time you run out of white stones. As you pull away from the river bank to the corner of the field continue in this line to find the next stile, then cut the corner of the field to the footbridge over Holden Beck. Bear left to the top of the rise to find a stile with a waymark then follow the fence above the river leaving it at a curve of the field to cut across to the band of trees. Then hold this line until you come to a farm access road, a pleasant lane fringed with blackberry bushes in autumn. Follow this to the road at Bolton-by-Bowland, turn right and wander through this very pleasant village which has an air of both tranquillity and antiquity.

This is hardly surprising as the village was listed in Domesday book and is one of the old settlements on the more fertile land at the edge of the Ribble valley. As its name suggests it was also on the very edge of the Forest of Bolland and was the administrative centre for the eastern part. It has two village greens, the smaller one on the Hellifield road having the well preserved village stocks and the stump of its market cross. The church stands at the junction of this road and the Gisburn road and is usually open from 11am. It's a very fine church compared with the other ancient churches in Bowland, probably reflecting the wealth of the Pudsay family of Bolton Hall whose head, Sir Ralph Pudsay, rebuilt it in 1466-7, though his grandson, Henry Pudsay built the South Chapel early in the sixteenth century. The splendid Pudsey Tomb lies between the two. It is a memorial to Sir Ralph who had three wives and twenty-five children. All of them, together with Sir Ralph's son William, who was Rector of the church at the time of its restoration, are depicted on its marble lid. Another, William Pudsay was an eccentric who minted his own coins from silver found in the lead from his mine at Rimington. Pursued by the military he escaped, it is said, by a prodigious leap on horseback across the Ribble at a spot known to this day as Pudsay's Leap.

Walk along the Gisburn road passing the church, the other village green and school. At the top of the hill ahead you will see a little gate in the fork of two roads and a footpath sign to the Gisburn road. Follow a line of mature trees on your right towards a short length of wall where you will find a stile, and continue in the same direction towards the right-hand end of the wood to find the next stile, a rather awkward one. A fine view of Pendle awaits you. Now go straight down the field towards the left of the farm buildings at Fooden and as soon as you cross the stile turn right past the farm buildings following the footpath signs (the path here has been diverted) to reach a wide shallow green track. Follow this track along the top side of the wood with glimpses of the Ribble below - if the trees allow - until the scene widens and you cross a little stream. Then bear right just a little as you cross the field to find the stile and then make towards the buildings entering a farm road by a gate.

Follow the farm road past the cottages and their outhouses, and after 200 yards, turn sharp left at the end of the wall onto a drive that goes through an ornamental stone gateway. This has an air of grandeur, for it was on the drive to Bolton Hall, demolished early this century. (If you don't fancy the ford keep straight on here to reach the road opposite the church and see the last paragraph.) You will pass through a bit of woodland then follow a walled section of the drive that opens out onto a lawn in front of a house. At the end of the wall turn sharp right onto a green cart-track that will take you into a field. Now take stock of things for ahead of you lies Skirden Beck, a sizeable stream that has to be forded at the right place. This is just to the right of a distant pair of trees and is in line with the footbridge over Holden Beck if you can spot that. A deep ditch and a fence bar direct access to the river and a short diversion left is needed. Then just splash across and continue to the top of the rise where you will find the footbridge you used on the outward walk. Cross it and re-trace your steps to Sawley.

Bolton-by-Bowland

Note: If there is too much water at the ford for your liking, retrace your steps to the ornamental gateway and continue up the drive to the road opposite the church. Turn left and pass through the village until you have crossed the road bridge over Skirden Beck then turn left down the farm access road and retrace your outward steps, taking care to leave the farm road where it swings left, crossing the stile straight ahead.

THE RIBBLE WAY FROM SAWLEY   Walk 5.2

The Ribble Way upstream from Sawley to within a mile or so of Gisburn is quite the finest stretch of the whole Way. Ideally you need a transport manager to pick you up at Gisburn where there is room to park by the toilets on the Bolton-by-Bowland road, and there is the possibility of a bus. Check at your local Tourist Information Office before you leave. Alternatively you can return via Bolton-by-Bowland.

Category:	B
Distance:	to Gisburn 4 miles, via Bolton-by-Bowland 9 miles
Time:	2 hours and 3½-4 hours respectively
Maps:	Pathfinder Series No.669 Chipping and Clitheroe and No.670 Barnoldswick and Earby (SD64/74 and SD84/94), though the latter is not essential
Start at:	Sawley, parking close to the pub for preference

Sawley to Gisburn

Go straight along the road from the pub towards the village of Sawley and where the road swings right up the hill keep straight ahead through the ornamental stone gateway onto the private road to Sawley Lodge, ignoring the threatening notice. As you approach a similar gateway turn left through a sheepfold into a field. After about 100 yards turn left across a bridge over a ditch into the field. Turn right and follow a line of stiles until you meet the river bank again at the entrance to Rainsber Wood. This section is very well waymarked, take care to follow it correctly as the owner of Sawley Hall is very sensitive to trespass.

You are now starting the finest part of the Ribble Way. Sometimes the path follows the river bank, sometimes it climbs quite steeply above it through the woods, sometimes through islands of pasture. Always it is utterly unspoilt, peaceful, serene, as the Ribble flows through this deep cut valley remote from the rest of the world. On a fine spring morning you may see the fish rising to fly, watch a waterhen shepherd her brood of coal black babies around the shallows, or be aroused from your day-dreams by the quack-quack of a pair of mallards. Take care you do nothing to mar this marvellous bit of riverside.

You will pass, on the opposite bank, Rainsber Scar, the limestone cliff down which Sir William Pudsey of Bolton Hall is said to have leapt on horseback to escape his pursuers. He was a coiner who made use of the silver extracted from the lead mined on his own estate at Rimington. He survived the leap and was eventually pardoned by Queen Elizabeth I.

Continue through this paradise until you reach a ladder stile, the first since entering the wood. Now bear right uphill, slightly away from the river. At first you follow a grassy bank that develops into a cart-track and when it ends you are on a grassy terrace above the river. Keep along it to find a stile on the right. Go up the field to cross a deep cut rivulet then turn left to follow the fence to the top side of the barn where you will find a stile. Cross it, turn left and follow the fence to the farm access road which you follow to a group of buildings. Turn left immediately before them to find a stile set back from the track. Now bear diagonally right to the field corner then left to drop down to a tiny stream which you cross and go through a wicket gate into a belt of woodland. As you emerge keep straight ahead to the stile to the left of the cottages, turn right on the farm road and right again when you reach the Boton-by-Bowland road. Ten minutes sees you in Gisburn.

The Return via Bolton-by-Bowland

When you reach the public road turn left and follow it, unfortunately, for about a mile. It's not too bad as there is the option of an excellent ice cream at Deer House Farm, and on the right just before the river bridge is the entrance to Gisburne Park where Lord Ribblesdale had his home. Gisburn Bridge it is quite scenic, for the river, partly hidden by trees, makes deep, dark, swirling pools below the road. Then it's a pull up the hill again, and a short mile to the start of the access road to Park House Farm. Pass the farm on its right and after crossing Park House Beck simply follow the fence to Fooden. Pass in front of the first set of buildings, turn right on the access road and continue through the farmyard and the gate to a stile. Head up the field to its right-hand corner to find the stile, then continue down the field to a short length of wall near the right-hand corner to find the next stile, and then follow the line of trees to the corner to find the stile onto the road. Turn left and follow the road right through the village to the bridge over Skirden Beck. Turn to Walk 5.1 to read something about this tranquil and attractive village.

As soon as you have crossed the bridge turn left onto a farm access road. Keep straight ahead in the corner where the road swings left and follow the fence to find the next stile then slant across the top of the wood and follow that steeply down to a stile where you turn right to find a good footbridge over Holden Beck. Turn left and after the first stile cross a long field to its right-hand corner and shortly reach the banks of the Ribble, if briefly. Now you follow a line of white splashed stones then trees to reach the stile by the road bridge.

Sawley Abbey

Whilst you are at Sawley you may care to have a look at the ruins of Sawley Abbey, sometimes known as Salley Abbey. At first sight there is little left above ground through extensive foundations have been excavated. The abbey was never wealthy like its parent house, for its lands were poor, and the climate harsh. This is reflected in the quality of the stonework, for there is very little ashlar masonry and large parts are simply built of rough stone blocks, some of it of the easily weathered Worston Shales, the cause of the gaunt appearance of the remains. It is still worth a look, however. It is maintained by English Heritage.

For the record, Sawley Abbey was founded in 1147, a daughter house of Fountains Abbey, not the nearby Whalley Abbey (which was founded in 1216, having been at Stanlow, Cheshire, before that date). Like other monastic houses it was dissolved in 1536 by Henry VIII and much of the better stone carted away to be used again, common practice in those days.

EASINGTON FELL FROM SAWLEY   Walk 5.3

The top of Easington Fell, 396m, can't be seen from Sawley, so it may never occur to you to climb it from there, yet it makes a better walk from Sawley than from Slaidburn. There is a good route through the fields, and right of way tracks take you to the last stile, within ¹/₄ mile of the summit cairn. Surely nobody is going to crib at that small distance to reach such a fine view point, arguably the best in the Bowlands? The return is via Waddington and the Ribble though it can be shortened by 2 miles by descending direct to West Bradford.

Category:	Just A if you use the right of way paths through the forest, B+ if you use the forest instead
Distance:	12 miles
Time:	5¹⁄₂-6¹⁄₂ hours
Map:	Pathfinder Series No.669 Chipping and Clitheroe (SD64/74)
Start at:	Sawley. See Walk 5.1 for parking.

Sawley to Scriddles Farm

Assuming you are parked on the north side of the bridge walk along the road to Grindleton for about 150 yards and turn right into the first lane on the right. It is signed the Friends Meeting House. At its end go through the gate and follow the little stream until you are just below the garden of Acreland, then cross it by a good footbridge and continue on the other side. Already there are pleasing views up the Ribble Valley. You will find whitewash splashes on the trees to keep you on the straight and narrow, but take care to go diagonally left from the first hedge corner to pick up the next splash and avoid the NO PATH sign staring you in the face if you do not. (The Sawley Estates at work again!) At least route finding is now easy. Simply follow these white splashes through three fields climbing quite steeply in parts and in the fourth one cut diagonally across to Till House. That's now the end of them. Pass to the left of the farm and go behind it to join their access road where you turn left and follow it through the buildings ahead. When you've passed a sharp left-hand corner by the next farm, look out for the stile in a wobbly fence opposite the last part of the house and continue straight up the field to the road at Scriddles Farm.

Now the view ahead and to the left is opening out. Pendle blocks all distant views to the south but westwards the lower Ribble Valley punctuated by the chimney of the Chatburn cement works opens out very pleasantly.

Scriddles Farm to the Summit

Turn left and in a few yards turn right into a short lane signed, "Footpath to Moor Lane". A well used tractor route left of the farmyard gets you started then head left for the gate and beyond it, the wall corner. Over the stile follow the wall/fence to its end to find a gate into the lane behind Higher Asker Hill Farm. Now head for a pleasant green track leading into the plantation where you keep straight ahead guided by white topped poles from time to time. In due course you emerge onto a road, a tarmac road, no less - and into a different scene.

This is the landscape of fells, of bracken and heather, whereas the other side of the plantation was verdant sheep pasture. Rarely does one get such a dramatic change, best experienced in spring and autumn when the browns and russets of the fell landscape offer the greatest colour contrast.

The road continues in a dead straight line up the fell. It looks a dreadful bore - and it is, *and* there's a lot more round the corner out of sight, but at least it's easy going which the right of way path is not, especially at the top, so take your pick.

By the road Eventually the road turns right at the top of the forest but a pleasant green track continues up the fell. Keep on this to the fork, from where there is a glimpse of a conical pile of stones on the near sky line. This is The Wife, Old Ned himself is further back. See Walk 2.2. Turn right at the fork and work your way up easily to a stile over a fence* where the green track ends. Immediately there is a stone step stile over the wall on the right. Cross this, follow the wall to the next stile, and as soon as you are over it the summit cairn is in view a short distance away.

By the right of way path Walk down the road for 200 yards and turn onto the forest road, third opening on the right. It winds about a bit and soon emerges from the forest, for there has been some extensive felling round here. As it emerges the start of the green track is on the left, besides a collapsed wall. This is the old right of way track, rough and wet in parts, but easily followed. Do just this until it emerges from the forest. Again a good deal of felling has taken place, in fact the whole of the upper part of the forest from below the old farm of Uplands seems to have been felled and some replanting was in progress in the spring of 1993. The green track continues however, and at the foot of the steep section you bear left, even though the better looking track goes right. It continues to the wall ahead where a stile puts you over an intervening fence into the bracken. Trample it down thoroughly, and continue up the fell following the wall until you come to the fence* mentioned above and continue to the top.

Easington Fell, a mere 396 metres, is quite isolated and therefore a superb view point. As you arrive at the cairn the whole of the Bowlands Fells that face south extends before you. Stocks Reservoir is easily picked up glinting in the sunshine. Slaidburn is well to its left, further left still a great wide V gap locates the Trough road and Dunsop Bridge. Behind to the left is the rounded end of Tottridge Fell and then not so easily distinguished, is the trio of Saddle, Wolf and Fair Snape Fells with Parlick a modest bump at the end. Beacon Fell can just be made out on the lower Ribble valley, then the eye leaps round to rest on the massive ridge of Pendle Hill. No mistaking the dominant hill of Ribblesdale, and forget it not, an outlier of the Forest of Bowland Area of Outstanding Natural Beauty. An undistinguished mass of low hills follows, then Embsay Moor and Fountains Fell lead the eye to Pen-y-Ghent and Ingleborough, the circuit well nigh complete.

The Summit to Waddington

Reverse your outward route over the last three stiles when you will pick up the green track you used if you came up the road. Simply follow it downhill, and in the dip below the gate by the scanty ruins of a building turn right. Now follow a rough cart-track across the field to a gate then head for the abandoned farm, Fell Side, ahead. As soon as you have passed it turn right and follow the wall over the fell to Moor Lane. There's a well trodden track. Turn left in the grassy walled lane and follow it down until you meet a tarmac lane at a corner. (If time is short you can keep straight on here down to the road on the outskirts of West Bradford where you join the main route.) Otherwise turn right on the road and follow it to Seedalls, then continue on the cinder track to Mill Farm on the other side of the deep cut, tree filled valley. Turn left down the side of the house and keep by the fence down to the stream to find the footbridge. Note that in spring 1993 some building work was in progress and the details here may change a little. Climb up out of the clough and then follow it down all the way to Waddington, except that when you come to a fence with a gate but no stile, turn left and then follow this fence to the road by the side of the Almshouses on the outskirts of Waddington, which is well worth a look. Turn right to reach the top of the village where there are toilets and a village shop.

Waddington is the most picturesque of the several villages in the Ribble valley that have a stream flowing down their middle. Waddington's is surrounded by its Coronation Gardens and is well worth a look. It has earned the title "Best Kept Village in Lancashire" on several occasions. The

Almshouses were originally built by a Robert Parker in 1700 for the poor widows of local men but have been rebuilt in their present location.

Waddington to Sawley

If you've wandered round Waddington retrace your steps and continue along the road until you reach the school where you have options. The start of the paths to West Bradford is completely blocked by houses and in any case is disputed, so this preferred route is not on. The path via Brungerley takes you out of your way quite a lot, so the preferred option may well be to continue along the road. As you approach the pub look out for a walled green track running down the side of the stream. This cuts off a bit of road and you rejoin it near the Ribble close to the stile. Turn left and follow the banks of the river, very pleasant grassy walking and well used, to the outskirts of Grindleton. When you are within sight of the village you reach a new waterworks road which is not shown on the map; just continue to follow the banks until you reach the start of a fenced track that runs behind Riverside Mill to the road. Turn right, go right again at the T-junction and at the corner of the bridge follow the Ribble Way to Sawley. First it runs along the flood banks of the river until it has passed the confluence of Swanside Beck then look for a stile in the hedge, turn right and when you meet the little brook turn right and follow it to the stile. Now go straight up the hill for two field lengths to find the stile onto the road. Turn right and follow the road for about a mile to find your car.

STARTING AT HURST GREEN

LONGRIDGE FELL AND THE HODDER   Walk 5.4

Very much an outlier of the Chipping area, this walk is still a worthy one. It starts at Hurst Green simply because of the difficulty of parking on the Chipping side of Longridge Fell, and crosses it away from the afforested end. After a length of road it returns by little used field paths to the road at Kemple End and reaches Hurst Green via the Hodder and the Ribble Way. It is only right to point out that the return along the Ribble is outside the Forest of Bowland but gives a far better route than returning along the road. The walk has exceptionally good and varied views as well as following a superb length of the Hodder. The shorter version returns via Stonyhurst and omits this length, but

Stonyhurst is very easily visited from Hurst Green as an extra by those who choose the Hodder and Ribble finish.

Category: B+ for the longer version, B for the shorter
Distance: 12¹/₂ miles or 8 for the shorter version
Time: 6 hours or 4¹/₂ for the shorter version
Maps: Pathfinder Series No.669 Chipping and Clitheroe and No.680
             Longridge and Great Harwood (SD64/74 and SD63/73)
Start at: Hurst Green. There is a layby on the Longridge-Clitheroe road on
             the Clitheroe side of the village.

Hurst Green to the Top of Longridge Fell

In the village turn right opposite the Shireburn Arms then walk up the road to the Bayley Arms. Almost opposite them turn down the lane on the left which ends at some stone built garages. The path continues on their right, joins a road that passes a house and continues into the wood besides the stream which it soon leaves to join an upper cart-track. The broad track which can be very muddy in parts, continues right through the wood then, having crossed the bridge, it leaves the wood and becomes a pleasant green lane. Bear right where it meets the farm access road and continue past Greengore, a very fine seventeenth-century building with triple buttresses supporting its east wall. The lane becomes grassy again and beyond the wood degenerates to a wet path following the wall. As compensation you will get your first view of Longridge Fell, clad in monotonous dark green conifers. After crossing a stile you will soon come to an isolated pair of stone gateposts. From them look up the hillside on the left and between the two clumps of trees you will see a ladder stile. This is where you are going. When you reach it turn round for the sake of the fine view towards Pendle. Once over it make diagonally right past the clumps of gorse to find a stile over the fence in the far corner. Continue in the same direction to join the road at a gate.

Turn left on the road and after about ¹/₄ mile turn right up a rough road with a large rather ornamental sign listing the properties it leads to. Go straight up it, it's a bit dull but doesn't last long, and when it turns right to Moor Game Hall keep straight on up the green lane which soon becomes a footpath. It is very well marked, simply follow it straight up the moor, cross a forestry road, and reach the wall that runs along the crest of Longridge Fell. A marvellous surprise view awaits you: the southern edge of the Bowlands from Beacon Fell to Totridge Fell. The summit cairn of Longridge Fell, 350m, named Spire Hill on the 1:25,000 map, is about 10 minutes walk to the right. The view is no better, but there is the satisfaction of going to the top.

Longridge Fell to Kemple End

Retrace your steps when you've visited the top and continue through the heather to the wide track down the steep northern escarpment. Towards the bottom the track forks and the most used route turns sharp left, but it is better to keep straight on through a bit of rough stuff - it shortens the road walking. When you've crossed the wall, go straight down to the road through a narrow field.

Turn right on the road, and after passing the drive to Rakefoot Farm turn into the fields on the right at the first footpath sign, a couple of minutes further on. At the top of the field a stile leads you into an old lane, unfortunately overgrown with bushes, blocked by fallen branches and waist high with nettles. It's completely impassable, the only thing to do is to walk the edge of the field. At its end a collapsed stile enables you to continue to follow the hedge and after wrestling with two more difficult stiles, to come in sight of the back of the pub, the Craven Heiffer, where you reach the road.

Turn right on the road and walk along it for almost a mile, passing the hamlet of Walker Fold with its tiny chapel and school. There are good views across the Hodder valley to relieve any boredom there may be and traffic is usually light. Eventually you will come to a footpath sign on the right and the route - there is no path until you come to the ruins of Chaigley Hall - goes through the gate immediately on its left. Go diagonally up the field keeping well above the line of the underground pipe and aim to reach the stream where the line of trees in the field ahead meets it, for the route continues *above* these trees. The stream is tiny but you'll have to duck under the single strand of wire to reach the gate into that field. Follow the hedge line through two fields, then move to the right to continue *below* the hedge line. As you approach the ruins of Chaigley Hall look out for a stile on the right and continue *above* the fence to the hall.

The ruins are not of some ancient mansion but of a double fronted house. The word "hall" merely indicates that it was a large house. It is believed that the original Chaigley Hall with its large barn was built around 1820-30, a time of agricultural expansion and improvement, but the ruins are probably those of a later Victorian house.

Do not go beyond the barn or you will be lost in a forest of nettles, but turn right keeping behind the house, and follow the fence to the wood. The route continues along the fence on a ridge of earth, once part of the access road to the hall, to reach the road at Kemple End.

This ridge gives superb views up the Ribble Valley, of Pendle and Clitheroe, and even, for the geologically minded, the bigger reef knolls, and although the Castle is not easy to pick out, the Chatburn Cement works stand bold and clear cut even on a day of poor visibility. There's a memorial seat at the best view point.

Turn left down the steep road and turn right through a gate with a public footpath sign after 5 or 6 minutes. This is the start of a very circuitous route through the fields which joins the riverside path about ¼ mile from Higher Hodder Bridge, but has good views and is preferable to the road which will take you direct to the bridge where the riverside footpath starts. From the roadside gate turn left through the lower of the two gates and half-way down the field bear right to a gate that puts you onto a farm access road. Follow this to Ryddings Farm, and in their yard look out for a stile on the left, rather than going through the little gate ahead. Now follow the fence down to the next stile where you turn sharp left to reach the bridge in the wood. A length of most welcome wooden walkway takes you across a mire then you follow the fence to reach a corner of the riverside path, which has been re-made with chippings and is in very good condition. Now turn right and simply follow this riverside path to Lower Hodder Bridge, at first in woodland poised high above the river, later on close cropped turf on the very banks of the river. In one place you have to climb a heart thumping double flight of steps and after only 100 yards or so go down a knee jolting double flight of steps to rejoin the river bank not far from the back of Hodder Place, a large house a bit like a mini-château. In all there's a couple of miles of superb river walking, the finest and final length of the Hodder, its swan song, as before you complete the walk you pass its confluence with the Ribble.

At Lower Hodder Bridge you will see the old bridge just below the present one: Cromwell is reputed to have crossed it when he passed this way. Have a look to see whether the footpath continues downstream, for it is planned to re-route the Ribble Way (which you have just joined) this way. If so, go that way for the very last bit of this superb river. If not, then turn right on the road and at the top of the hill turn left into the fields close to an electricity substation. Bear left in the first field to find the stile, slightly right in the second large field to join the access road to Winckley Hall close to a red roofed building. Follow this road right through the buildings down to the bank of the Hodder. Just ahead you will see its confluence with the Ribble, and as you approach the curve of the river, you will see Hacking Hall, one of the many venerable houses of Ribblesdale, on the opposite bank. Continue along this not very attractive cart-track until it swings away to the right just past Jumbles Farm and then keep straight on until you reach a large chunk of woodland on the river banks. Here Ribble Way signs point you to a footbridge then a well trodden path through the first part of the wood. Then it goes left across the top of the wood to join the access road to Trough Farm where you turn right and follow this track up to the road at Hurst Green near the Shireburn Arms. Turn right to find your car.

About Hacking Hall

This venerable house appears in the Coucher Book of Whalley Abbey of 1374, but the present house was rebuilt in 1607 by Thos Walmsley, then in his 70th year. He lived at Dunkenhalgh near Clayton-le-Woods at the time and built it for his wife so that she could have her own residence after his death. It has been called the house of many gables - there are five under the front roof line. The projecting wings, mullioned windows and massive chimney breast on the south wall give it a most attractive appearance. Naturally it had its own ferry across both the Ribble and Calder and the ferry man lived in the house opposite, now derelict. This ferry ran until 1954 and was of considerable value to walkers in the area. One of its old boats was discovered in a barn in 1983 and has been restored and is now in Clitheroe Castle Museum. This particular boat was about 12ft long and could take 15 passengers, and was in use until 1938 when it was replaced.

The short return: Kemple End to Hurst Green via Stonyhurst

When you reach the road from Chaigley Hall track, go straight across it into a gravel track, bear right in front of the row of very attractive houses, then left past more houses to reach a muddy farm lane. At its end in the field bear left downwards to the hedge to find the stile and continue to the next stile 50 yards ahead on the right. Then cut across to the house, Throstle Nest, where you will pick up their access road.

Follow it to the public road, turn right, and where it makes a sharp turn right, turn left down the private road leading to Stonyhurst College. The road passes between the front of the college and its twin lakes, too close for the best view of this noble building, but it is no hardship to go to the end of the lakes for the classic view of Stonyhurst with its twin cupolas. Go straight past the house, continue along the road that leads to the car park, and when you reach the playing fields turn right into the field. A broad well trodden track takes you towards the wood, then follow the fence through several fields into the top end of Hurst Green just above the Shireburn Alms houses.

These Alms houses originally stood on the Longridge road about ¹/₂ mile from Kemple End and were built by one of the Shireburn family in 1707. They had become derelict after World War II and were removed and rebuilt stone by stone in their present location by the Lancashire County Council in 1946.

Turn left and a few minutes sees you at your car.

About Stonyhurst College

The college is a well known Roman Catholic public school and has been at Stonyhurst since 1794. The college was founded in France in Henry VIII's time in order to offer English Catholics the type of education denied them in England. During the French Revolution the college experienced considerable difficulties in France, so the Weld family of Dorset who had inherited the Stonyhurst property, offered it to the school which had just lost its own house. Stonyhurst has a very long history. Sir Richard Shireburn began to build a new house in 1592 and the present Gatehouse is part of it and can be seen quite well as you pass. Generations of the family continued to live there, each making additions or alterations until the family died out in 1717 with the death of Sir Nicholas Shireburn. He was the man who built the two big cupolas, a landmark for miles around, and laid out the ornamental lakes and grounds at the back of the college.

Obviously the new owners of Stonyhurst started a repair and building programme to suit their needs. In the mid nineteenth century there was a boom in public school building and the next forty years saw the buildings completed as we see them today, though the church was built between 1832 and 1835. The school houses a museum which contains priceless relics of Renaissance times and a library with some very rare books. It is open to the public in July and August, daily except Mondays, for a small charge.

SOURCES

Barratt, *Directory of Preston and Fylde District 1898*

Bolton, C. & Greenwood, M. *Bolland Forest and the Hodder Valley* published privately

Boyd Dawkins, *Lancashire and Cheshire Antiquarian Society 1890 Vol XVIII p.114*

Catlow, R. *Ribble Valley rendezvous* Countryside Publications Ltd

Evans, J. *The Ward's Stone of Bowland* Bowland Books

Freethy, R. *Exploring Bowland and the Hodder* Countryside Publications Ltd

Garnett, E. *Friends in Wray* printed privately

Johnson R.H. (ed.) *The Geomorphology of North-West England* Manchester University Press

Dixon, J. & Järvinen, J. *Historic Walks around Bleasdale* Carnegie Press, Preston

Dixon, J. & Järvinen, J. *Historic Walks around the Forest of Bowland* Carnegie Press, Preston

Graystone, P. *Walking Roman Roads in Bowland* Centre for North West Regional Studies, University of Lancaster

Lord, A.A. *Wandering in Bowland* Westmorland Gazette

Lofthouse, J. *Three Rivers* Robert Hale Ltd

Margary, Ivan D. *Roman Roads in Britain* John Baker

Mitchell, W.R. *Bowland and Pendle Hill:* a Tourist's Guide, Dalesman Publishing Co., Clapham

Ovenell, T. *Walks in the Forest of Bowland* Frederick Warne

Parker, S. *Brock Bottoms: a History of the Mill and the Community* Lancashire County Books

Pevsner, N. *The Buildings of England: North Lancashire* Penguin Books

Rothwell E. & C. *The River Wyre: People and Places* printed privately

Shaw, R.C. *The Royal Forest of Lancaster* published privately

Tattersall, D. *Forest of Bowland, An Area of Outstanding Natural Beauty: Statement of Intent* Lancashire County Council

Various *The Geology of the Country around Clitheroe* HMSO

Various *The Geology of the Country around Settle* HMSO

Whittaker's Almanac 1985

Wray, D.A. *British Regional Geology: The Pennines and Adjacent Areas* HMSO

Winchester A. (ed.) *Bleasdale in the Nineteenth Century* unpublished

Maps

British Geological Survey 1:50,000 Sheet 68 Clitheroe

British Geological Survey 1:50,000 Sheet 67 Garstang

Yates Map of Lancashire 1786

PRINTED BY CARNMOR PRINT & DESIGN
95/97 LONDON ROAD, PRESTON, LANCS